ON BECOMING WHOLE IN CHRIST

ON BECOMING WHOLE IN CHRIST
An Interpretation of the *Spiritual Exercises*

John F. X. Sheehan, S.J.

Loyola University Press
Chicago, IL 60657

To the Memory
of
Thomas Edward Sheehan
and
Theresa Ellen Kiely Sheehan
Who Loved to Pray

© 1978 Loyola University Press
Printed in the United States of America

LIBRARY OF CONGRESS
CATALOGING IN PUBLICATION DATA

Sheehan, John F X

   On becoming whole in Christ.

   Reprint of ed. published by Dimension Books,
Denville, N. J.

   1.   Loyola, Ignacio de, Saint, 1491-1556.   Exercitia
spiritualia.   2.   Spiritual exercises.   I.   Title.

BX2179.L7S47   242   78-9936

ISBN 0-8294-0278-0

TABLE OF CONTENTS

Foreword by Egon W. Gerdes
Preface

Part I

I. Preamble 10
II. A Parable 13
III. "The evil that men do . . . " 19
IV. The Personality of Christ 24
V. "And the Word was Made Flesh" (Jn. 1:14) 30
VI. "Is this not the carpenter's son?". . .' (Mt. 13:55) .37
VII. A Contemplation on Choice 43
VIII. Degrees of Commitment 47
IX. Like Unto Christ 52
X. Suffering 57
XI. Prayer, Eucharist, and Death 62
XII. "And they led him to Caiphas" 66
XIII. Greater Love than this 71
XIV. Arise My Love 76

Part II

Spiritual Exercises
and
Author's Commentary

FOREWORD

The ecumenical movement must be making progress. A Protestant theologian is writing a Foreword to a Catholic book in spirituality.

This is not a work which reflects, merely intellectually, on spirituality. It is dealing in spirituality, an invitation to enrich the spiritual life by walking, through the guidance of the author, with a master of the spiritual life, Ignatius of Loyola.

Spiritual pilgrimages twist and wither when gone alone. We all need direction. If no saintly person is around to help us, this work is as good a substitute as any to be found.

A Protestant, and a Methodist at that, warmly recommends this little book of a Catholic on a Catholic, both Jesuits. I have myself long been searching for spiritual help and have found it hard to come by these days, especially among Protestants. Where does one turn for counsel to grow in the life of the Holy Spirit? Who can unfold the spiritual riches of the Christian tradition from a Protestant perspective? Most who try seem to be on the fringes, more behind than ahead, be they fundamentalist or spiritualist. Where is ecumenical help? I personally first went back in my history, following the Wesleys to the Puritans, and discovered that they in turn had learned from the Jesuits. I then thought that the time might be ripe to claim, among many other Catholic saints, also Ignatius for our pedigree as well.

The Wesleys were trying to hold together, as they said, knowledge and vital piety. In that they reverberate Ignatius'

scriptural concern for piety, Father Sheehan, our guide
and Ignatius' spokesman, rightly apologizes for neither
knowledge of scripture or piety.

All of this is probably something like a belated
rationalization for my praying through the Ignatian Spiritual Exercises when I needed guidance most. I found my
director within the Jesuit tradition of spirituality. I will
always gladly confess my indebtedness.

Why spiritual exercises? Isn't a spiritual encounter
enough? Exercises are the means to enhance spiritual
growth. The Wesleys devised a whole organizational system
of conventicles, of societies, classes and bands for this
purpose. In them Christian spirituality could be corpo-
rately cultivated and mutually corrected, even beyond the
minimal relationship of a spiritual director and the person
in his or her care.

Whoever looks for more than an isolated encounter, for
something else than a quick, instant panacea, once and for
all decision solution to problems of the spiritual life is
invited to give Ignatius a fair hearing. Such an enterprise is
made so much easier through the skillful direction of
Father Sheehan.

The skillfulness appears when we follow a warmhearted
exegete at work. He knows how to clear rubble away from
the text of Ignatius so as to let it shine in new splendour.
What finally shines through is the text of Holy Scripture
itself, made dear again in lucid style. If the readers do not
care much for a companion volume to Ignatius' Exercises
—although they certainly would profit by that alone—then
let them at least enjoy the refreshing reflections on
Scripture. In rediscovering Scripture the Catholics have
truly become Protestant.

Can Protestants move closer to the Catholics? Certainly. The first step on the way will be taken if we do not misunderstand this work as preaching about Scripture but understand it as meditating on Scripture. Ignatius and his interpreter kindly request from us—and I for one have followed the advice with great blessing—not just to read through the booklet, but to meander, to stop and go, to reflect, to let the mind wander as the heart ponders. If the readers do this they are in for a spiritual trip in the best sense of the word.

Egon W. Gerdes
Professor of Historical Theology
Garrett-Evangelical Theological Seminary,
Evanston, IL
Director of Protestant Spirituality
Ecumenical Institute of Spirituality
in America,
Evanston, IL

PREFACE

Authors who send books out to the world feel an emotion felt otherwise only by the mothers of small children facing the second day of kindergarten. The first day she could accompany the child, but now he must confront the world all alone. We can only hope that our children are met kindly.

This is an unrepentantly pious book. The word "pious" is unfortunate perhaps. The word fell among bad companions in recent decades and like most who do, it has ended badly. But there is no other word. By using it I mean that the thrust of the book is derived from a conviction that there is a better world than the one in which we now move and that the realities of that world certainly color this one. We are so preoccupied with the present world that if we do not occasionally contemplate the realities of the other, those realities will not influence us.

It is hoped that the book represents a sturdy piety. While the book is not a work of scholarship, the author has tried to let no line slip by that is at strong variance with the demands of modern scholarship. Piety, the Jesuit theologian Suarez once noted, is feeble without scholarship. And he could have added, it certainly has nothing to fear from scholarship.

This modest work was written over a long period of time in hours stolen from other chores. It was finished in Uppsala, Sweden. It is a pleasant task to thank the Jesuit Community there for making the completion possible. It was begun in Milwaukee, Wisconsin. It is a pleasure also to thank that Jesuit community for many years of affective support. Fathers Burns, Caldwell, and Walsh have manifested that support in a variety of practical ways. Finally, the author thanks Miss Diane Bajczyk who joins great skills in typing and proof-reading to a lively personality and unfailing cheerfulness.

John F. X. Sheehan
August 15, 1975

I

PREAMBLE

At the height of a distinguished career in psychology, Carl Rogers wrote that he did not know how or why "client-centered" therapy worked. He did know, however, that people came to him in this therapy, reflected in his presence, thought out loud with his encouragement and were—in some mysterious fashion—improved. They left him to lead richer, more human lives. Retreat directors feel somewhat the same way about the *Spiritual Exercises*. The structured retreat is clearly successful beyond any success due the sum of its parts. People who make structured retreats seem much improved. They consistently leave the retreat with greater strength to face the rigors of a living Christianity in a harsh world. To many directors, this greater strength seems more than is normally derived from other forms of prayer, reflection and spiritual activity.

For this reason, directors are delighted at the opportunity to present the Exercises under many formats. They can be given over a period of thirty full days (not too practicable for most of us) or eight days. These forms are generally given in seclusion. But the demand for the *Exercises* under more practicable circumstances has led to a retreat given one night a week over a period of some months. They can be made with or without a director. In the latter case, of course, the exercitant needs a proper book.

It is for this last person that this book is written. The book envisions a person far from a retreat house in a busy city or rural seclusion, praying alone or with others, with or without the assistance of any clergyman skilled in spiritual counsel. If there is the opportunity for a small group to assemble in someone's home for prayerful discussion of what the book contains, so much the better; "If two or three are gathered in my name . . ."(Mt. 18:20).

Perhaps more than any other Christian teacher of prayer, St. Ignatius saw the uselessness of trying to suppress the imagination in a life of contemplation. He calls on his disciples regularly to make use of their imagination, to see, hear, feel, taste, to make of their prayer a truly human experience. The *Exercises* grew out of St. Ignatius' own life experience. As a result of his own prayer in the Cave at Manresa, he came from leading a rather ordinary life to one of complete dedication to the Gospel. Afterwards, putting together the meditations that had led him to reject the ordinary for a better life, he saw as the purpose of the *Exercises* that they would help "in making a decision and bringing order into one's life." The Exercises then can be of assistance in making major life decisions.

Fortunately, most of us do not have to make major life decisions regularly. Yet, it is a rare dedicated Christian who does not wonder from time to time if his life ought not to be in better harmony with the Gospel. For such a person also were the *Exercises* written. Ignatius saw such a person as specially open to the voice of the Spirit. The Spirit's direction then was to be weighed in the four "weeks" of the Exercises. These portions of the Exercises encourage the Christian to weigh any possible decision on life improvement in light of Reason, the example of Christ's Public Life, Passion and Death, and Risen Life. Such "decision-making" is not to be a conscious preoccupation of the *Exercises*. Ignatius judged that the Spirit would speak clearly and directly to the Christian who made these contemplations on the meaning of the Gospel. In the ideal order, the nature of any "decision" to be made ought to be vaguely understood by the end of the "week" of reflection on Christ's public life. Subsequent "weeks" are designed to strengthen any decision that has to be made.

Perhaps the reader feels that the use of this book is not the ideal way to approach the Divinity. He compares the possibility of private reading or weekly gatherings to a month alone in a Trappist monastery and feels somewhat discouraged. He should resist such discouragement! If the Christian traditions are in agreement on anything, they agree on this: when the Christian is inspired to approach the Divinity in love and humility, the Divinity will come to meet him where he is, however far away, however difficult the circumstances. St. Ignatius wrote that God dealt with him "as a schoolteacher with a child." This phrase has been badly misunderstood by older commentators who read their own stern cultures into Ignatius' life. Ignatius had happy memories of the Basque tutor, a member of the household, who led him with affection (and gifts of warm chestnuts) from ignorance into a semblance of learning. It is a Christian conviction that the disciple who admits his ignorance finds the Divinity to be such a schoolteacher.

The Essays that follow are designed for thorough reflection rather than brisk perusal. If the reader finds a single idea in an essay to be very satisfying, he should be content to reflect on the single thought without concern for finishing the Essay in whatever time he has allotted himself. The Spirit does not hasten and will not be hurried.

Finally, it should be noted that this book is divided into two overall portions. The chapters of Part I are an *interpretation* of the Spiritual Exercises. They represent a personal effort to put sinew and flesh on the skeleton of the *Exercises* as Ignatius wrote them. Part II is the Exercises themselves, not so much in translation as in paraphrase and adaptation. The written version of the *Exercises* as we have it is almost unintelligible to the beginner. It is a collection of terse jottings by a man who was not terribly fluent and literate in his writings. Occasionally the poetic soul of Ignatius bursts forth in song. In large measure, though, his written account of the *Exercises* is composed in a kind of pedestrian shorthand.

The effort of our paraphrase is to combine translation and implicit commentary. It strives to be faithful enough to Ignatius' mind that the reader may use it, eventually, to create his own interpretation of what Ignatius taught. This the reader should attempt, though, only after he has reflected prayerfully on the interpretation which constitutes Part I.

II

A PARABLE

Some Christians have found the following modern parable helpful as it echoes the emotions which they have experienced in coming to lead a deeper Christian life:

"Imagine yourself under the happiest of circumstances; in the home of a good friend and surrounded by a number of acquaintances. It is winter and you stand before a roaring fire, perhaps with a drink in your hand, chatting with the group and smelling the delicious odors of a dinner being prepared. The host pauses in the doorway and announces happily, "Sue says dinner will be ready in about ten minutes." You notice that the light snow of the late afternoon has turned heavy now, and you reflect that it is good to be inside the house, warm, about to be fed—and with company. And you hear a voice, quiet but insistent, and it tells you: 'Put on your hat and coat and go out into the storm and keep walking. Sometime, somewhere, I shall meet you.' And you put on your hat and coat and you leave everything."

Many Christians in a wide variety of traditions find this parable sympathetic. With all the joy with which they reflect on their baptism and, in many traditions, their first communion, they think of their real commitment to Christianity as anchored to some adult action. For clergymen and religious, the moment in time is sometimes easier to pinpoint; it was tied to ordination, or religious profession. For some married Christians, it was the marriage ceremony that marked the beginning of a solid, adult, religious commitment. In some religious traditions, the moment of "decision for Christ" could be tied to a knife-edge moment of time in a particular place. But for almost all adult Christians, there is some period, perhaps vague, in one's past life which marks a watershed, a Before and an After. The After was characterized by a deeper commitment, a greater reliance on faith, and the hearing of a promise that says "sometime, somewhere, I shall meet you." The moment of meeting is long delayed. When a meeting occurs it is ecstatic—but brief. The voice is heard no more and the memory of the last words remain, "keep on moving and I shall meet you again."

Abraham

The parable of course, is little other than a faintly disguised version of the story of Abraham which the Bible relates in Genesis 12, 15 and 22. Abraham was a bedouin sheik who really made no exorbitant demands on life. He wanted land, water, and—above all—posterity. In a world with views of immortality which were murky at best, the yearning for offspring was more intense than in any other age. One's children were one's immortality. The desire to live long enough to see the children of one's children was not simply a desire to lead a long life. By seeing one's own offspring with children of their own was to be convinced that the proper procedure was continuing, to know that those small children would then someday also beget children. Thus would one be assured of a kind of immortality.

As the Old Testament relates it, Abraham did have some land and water where he was. Still, at the word of the Lord, he moved out from the land of his fathers in search of another yet unknown. No longer a young man, and with a wife no longer young, he remonstrated mildly with the Lord that the Divine promises of a posterity to him were quite impossible. "Look toward heaven and number the stars if you are able . . . So shall your descendants be" (Gen. 15:5). And the Old Testament tells us that Abraham "believed" and so entered into the realm of the righteous.

The word "believe" in both Old and New Testaments has a connotation which the English translation has lost. The sharp edges of the word have been dulled by long usage. The New Testament *pisteuein* and the Old Testament *leheamin* mean rather, "trust." Both words involve a leap, a movement into the dark, relying on something unseen. They involve decisions based on confidence in the word of the speaker. "And Abraham leaped into trust and was thus counted among them that are justified."

The Divinity watched over Abraham and kept in close contact with him. Abraham prospered in everything. A child was born who grew up healthy and strong. Abraham loved the child as parents love only those children born after they have given up hope of offspring. But children are dangerous gifts. A man's love for his children (like any relationship of human love) carries with it the inbuilt fear of separation. On the death of his infant son, President Kennedy sadly quoted to a friend a French proverb: "He who marries and has children has given hostages to fortune."

Abraham had no such fears. Isaac was after all the gift of the Lord and would be the Divinity's instrument in granting him immortality through offspring. But the Lord spoke again to Abraham: "Take your only son Isaac whom you love and go to the land of Moriah and offer him there as a burnt offering upon one of the mountains which I shall show you" (Gen. 22:2).

Even a poor imagination can reconstruct the scene as Abraham and Isaac make their journey to the distant mountain. Isaac has been told only that they are to offer a sacrifice and at some point in the journey he alertly inquires, "Father, we have wood and fire, but where is the animal for the burnt offering?" (Gen. 22:7). Abraham replies only, "the Lord will provide, my son." A Jewish tradition insists that at this point, Isaac knew what was afoot. The journey continues in silence.

The story, of course, has a "happy ending." The Lord

intervenes and assures Abraham that the command was given only as a test and Abraham had passed it easily. But the "happy endings" of such stories in the patriarchal narratives, in the lives of the saints, or the lives of great contemporary Christians, do not make those stories less helpful or encouraging to us. Christianity itself has a happy ending. Christ did rise!

How God is Best Approached

St. Ignatius insists throughout his retreat that a proper mood is required when one approaches the Divinity in prayer. For Ignatius this proper mood is deeply tinged with awe. He rarely speaks of God the Father without describing him as "the Divine Majesty." From this attitude, Ignatius is insistent that one does not rush into prayer, but takes a moment or two to collect oneself before entering into the presence of the Lord. Ignatius, as generally, stands on a good scriptural tradition here. Exodus 3 narrates the first meeting of the Divinity with his chosen Moses. From this meeting, as the Old Testament tells the story, were to result the Exodus, the formation of the nation of Israel, and all subsequent Judaeo-Christian history. After calling Moses by name, the Divinity gives him some advice on how the Lord is to be approached in prayer. "Take off your shoes, for the place on which you stand is holy ground. And come no closer!" (Ex. 3:5).

This awesomeness of the Lord is sometimes difficult for modern Christians to grasp. Most Christian traditions include notions of the Lord's distance and proximity. The Divinity is awesome, other, and remote, and yet the Spirit dwells in us. The Divinity is an awful judge, but the

Incarnate Lord is an exhaustible source of mercy. Humans grow weary with contradictions and every age and every person is tempted to make choices of its own—Justice or Mercy, Transcendance or Immanence. Ignatius is too wise for this. He retains all the contradictions. So far is the Divinity above our understanding that he is best understood (to the extent that humans can understand Him) by consecutive statements of apparent contradictions with little attempt at reconciliation of the conflict.

Ignatius offers much advice on the manners of prayer in the course of his little work. We shall interpolate some of it from time to time in our essays. One point must be mentioned at the beginning. Ignatius is a bit of a spiritual pragmatist. He encourages us to "do what works" when we pray. If the question under discussion is our posture in prayer, our diet in time of prolonged prayer, the books we use, whether we speak aloud or silently, whether we meditate on the Divine Truths with the use of words or contemplate a single image, Ignatius asks only one question: does it work? does it make our prayer apparently more easy and profitable?

And here we may be encouraged to a little personal boldness. A biographer of El Greco has remarked that when he began to paint his strange figures, with their oddly draped clothing and elongated shapes, surely a number of people must have said to him, "great painters do not paint that way." But El Greco replied either openly to them or quietly to himself, "But I do. I paint this way." If we are to be successful in prayer we must share a bit of the artist's boldness, with confidence in the temperament that the Divinity has given us and confident of his personal leading in a manner suited to our God-given psyches.

III

"THE EVIL THAT MEN DO . . ."

An American weekly magazine recently did an article on "The Liberated Woman." The article offered many fine examples of the effect of modern "liberation" on America's women along with one unfortunate illustration. It cited the rise in the number of middle-class mothers with small children who had simply walked away from husband and family in quest of a career. The article presented this as an act of great courage on the part of these women and described it also as something "modern" which could not have happened in an earlier age. Reader reaction was quick. One woman wrote back: "There is nothing modern about this. My great-grandmother abandoned husband and children in 1880 because she desired to do her thing. She died, unmourned, after two decades, but the harmful consequences of her action have lasted to the fourth generation."

This is a harsh statement and we could not simply endorse it. We do not know, generally, why people do things. And after all, it is largely motivation that makes an action right or wrong. Still, this one angry reader had attained one insight. Actions have consequences. If the action is evil, frequently the consequences are evil. The consequences set into motion by a single act may live generations after the death of the person who began the chain.

Perhaps Ignatius knew this from other sources, but it is likely that this is one more lesson he learned from his reading of the Old Testament. The Hebrew word *'awon* is used in the Old Testament for *sin*. It is also used indifferently for *guilt, punishment,* or *consequences* (even to the innocent) that are associated with a given sinful act. For the world of the Old Testament, the matter is very clear. There is little point in distinguishing between sinful *act* and all that follows it. Whatever follows sin is hopelessly entangled with the sin that preceded; there is nothing gained, says the Old Testament, in attempting to separate the one from the other. Ignatius is writing in this same mode. Sin produces *consequences* and the consequences affect not simply the individual but the community.

The communitarian aspect of sin and its consequences must be stressed or a vital point of the *Exercises* may be lost. But vital points of the *Exercises* are easily lost; Ignatius was a very poor writer. His thoughts (we have every reason to believe) soared to the heavens; his prose was quite earthbound. To understand Ignatius, the scholar working in the *Exercises* must research a variety of traditions which stand outside the *Exercises* but complement them. One scholar of the *Exercises* in the nineteenth century, Jan Roothaan, failed to do just that. As a result, in his Latin translation of the *Exercises* (which had enormous significance until our own lifetime), Ignatius comes across not as the warm-hearted, gentle Basque that he was, but as the dour, legalistic Dutch cleric that Roothaan was!

In reading the *Exercises*, we must always be alert to what Ignatius implies, along with what he says. In treating the notion of Sin, he does eventually suggest that we meditate on the sins of our past life. We shall come to that eventually. But first we must examine the two suggestions which precede the meditation on "Personal Sin" and which set the tone for it.

Ignatius wants us to contemplate the "Sin of the Angels" and the "Sin of Adam and Eve." Christian teaching to the days of Ignatius had placed great stress on the notion of "the Fall of the Angels." The traditions of this fall varied, but their common denominator was clear. The angelic host was offered an opportunity to decide for or against the Divinity and some of them chose wrongly. Ignatius stresses the consequences that followed from the sin—as Christian teaching saw it. The angelic chieftain, Lucifer, the "Illuminator," became Satan, "The Enemy"; half the angelic host became hostile to man now and no longer helpful. "And all this," Ignatius repeats frequently, "for a single serious sin." Ignatius, like all great religious leaders, is a mixture resulting from his charismatic insight and cultural conditioning. Ignatius Loyola—Theologian and Exegete—was very much a child of his own time. But his basic insight here is sound. Sin affects not only the individual, but the community.

In his reflection on Adam and Eve, Ignatius had better instincts than some people writing on the subject in our lifetime. Ignatius had no difficulty in imagining a primeval sin with consequences lasting to his own day. The modern mind has no better solution for the "problem of Evil" than that of Adam and Eve, but tends to reject the account because twentieth century individualism finds it incomprehensible. For this reason, the Adam and Eve account (Genesis 3) which is somewhat familiar to all of us is best studied in the context of some other Old Testament accounts which may not be so familiar.

The core mystery of the Adam and Eve account—that a single sin can harm all mankind—is reflected (among other places) in the episode of Jonathan's "taste of honey." Engaged in violent combat with the enemies of Israel, King Saul vows that no one of his warriors will taste food until the victory is in hand (I Samuel 14:24-52). His beloved son Jonathan never hears the command and at one point touches the tip of his staff into a supply of wild honey and swallows it. Shortly thereafter cruel punishment descends on all the hosts of Israel. By a process of divination, it becomes clear that Jonathan is guilty of "sin" and under questioning he admits his tasting of the honey. Only the intercession of the people saves him from death at his father's hands.

The story is mysterious—as is much of the Old Testament. The notion of the "hidden sin," the possibility of gravely offending the Divinity and yet having no knowledge of one's offense, has not lived on in Christianity. (But even this notion enhances the greatness and remoteness of the Divinity. What has lived on throughout the rest of Hebrew history and into Christian times is that the individual cannot sin without harming the human family, since the family is one. All of us have protested in self-defense from time to time, "I am only hurting myself." The world of the Old Testament would reject this summarily. It is impossible to hurt oneself without hurting all mankind. For the Old Testament, the idea that no man is an island is so clear a principle as to need no proof.

Only after these reflections does Ignatius bring us to contemplate our own sins. They are not to be contemplated as something apart from the history of the human family. If we have failed in the past, in thought or activity, the world is today less holy as a result; God's grace is somehow less present among men by reason of our failure. If we desire to lead better lives in the future, our motivation is very imperfect if we wish only to be better individuals. Rather, Ignatius would have us envision a human family more like the image of Christ if we shore up what is lacking in our own Christianity.

We must be very careful in meditating on our own past sins. If we are not careful, such meditation can be a process by which we ourselves, and not the Divinity, become the central focus of the *Exercises*. Rather we should contemplate our past sins (briefly) from this viewpoint: each sin has been the occasion of a special gift of the Divinity; each one has given us a particular share in the saving work of Christ; each has given us a particular reason to be grateful to Christ for making us His own.

If we spend a few moments in such contemplation, we shall be ready for what Ignatius calls "Conversations" as a form of prayer. We are to converse with the Divinity, "as a friend speaks to a friend whom he has offended, as a servant speaks to his master." And Ignatius seems confident that the Divinity will speak back to us. Is this possible?

Indeed it is. One gifted writer on the Exercises quotes at this juncture, G. B. Shaw's *St. Joan*. She has told a skeptic that she hears God speaking to her in voices and he objects that these are not voices, but her own imagination. She answers: "Of course! How else does God speak to us except through our imagination." For those of us who believe in a loving, creating God, it is no puzzle that the Divinity can speak in such fashion. The Divinity knows what is in man, as he has placed it all there. He moves gracefully and easily in the midst of all that is the human lot, using imagination and passion, physical strengths and weaknesses, the realm of the healthy psyche and the weak one, to speak to all of us who try to listen.

IV

THE PERSONALITY OF CHRIST

The late Daniel Lord, S.J., was a man of many parts: a gifted writer and sometime dramatist with some theological training as a Jesuit. The combination made him attractive to Cecil B. DeMille, who hired him as a technical adviser on his first production of *The King of Kings*. Fr. Lord relished the assignment—to a point. DeMille conceived the idea that the movie could be embellished with one sub-plot, a passionate love affair between Mary Magdalen and Jesus, and Fr. Lord was having small success in dissuading him. Then, on a given morning, the two sat together watching a brief scene starring H. B. Warner, the lead of the movie. In the scene, Warner recited a few lines from the gospels showing Jesus in his dealings with persons. At its conclusion DeMille turned to Lord and remarked with excitement, "He is great, isn't he?" Fr. Lord was surprised as he considered Warner to be an actor of limited gifts. "Warner?" he asked with some wonder in his voice. "No," said DeMille, "Jesus. Jesus is great!" And in that moment, recalls Fr. Lord, there died the idea of the embellished sub-plot.

Some may find the above story banal and be affronted by the Hollywood-style language, "Jesus is great!" Still, there is a point to the story that is important at this juncture in the *Exercises*. Such is the power of the personality of Christ that it can reach men under the poorest of circumstances—as here through a few lines of the gospel recited by a second-rate actor—and can change men's views. This is, of course, the major thrust of the *Exercises*. It is an effort to allow the personality of Christ so to reach into our lives that those lives will never again be the same. From this point on, the exercises are little more than a carefully guided contemplation of the life of Christ viewed from certain perspectives. If we are profitably to follow the exercises we must settle on a few "ground-rules."

Ignatius contemplated the gospels in the light of the very best modern scholarship which his lifetime had to offer. (We tend to think of Ignatius as unlettered, perhaps by reason of the limited literary caliber of the Exercises. Such an image of him is false. In an age of limited education he had an M.A. from the University of Paris). We too, then, must contemplate the gospels in the light of the best sound scholarship which our age has to offer.

And our age offers us a great deal. Sometimes, led on by a brief newspaper account summarizing what some reporter thought a scholar has said, we tend to regard scholarship as destructive of faith. This is quite false. The best of sound, modern biblical scholarship gives our age a richer view of the Gospel message than has ever been available before.

For example, modern scholars have enriched our knowledge of symbolism in Scripture. Some are inclined to think that given realities in the New Testament can be written off as "only a symbol"; rather, many symbols in the New Testament cover deeper and hidden realities which cannot be touched until the symbol is explored. A good example

of this can be found in the gospel accounts of the Baptism
of Jesus. Matthew, Mark, Luke and John agree that a dove
descended on Jesus in the course of the Baptism (Mt. 3.16,
Mk. 1.10, Lk. 3.22, Jn. 1.32). Later Christian tradition has
been unanimous in portraying the Spirit as a dove, and
most Christian readers of the gospels are content to rest
with the single image. But there is more here.

The dove makes a specific appearance in the account of
Noah and the flood (Gn. 8:8-12). Moreover, the dove
appears here in connection with the waters of the flood,
themselves a symbol of unleashed chaos. One of the Old
Testament accounts of creation hints at a dove, too. The
Spirit of God "flutters" (*merahepheth* in Hebrew) over the
deep, chaotic waters. It is from this verb that early Hebrew
symbolism came to picture the Spirit of God as a dove. It
was their symbolism, of course, that the early Christians
adopted.

See then what modern scholarship adds to this contemplation. It does not detract from the beautiful portrait of
Christ submitting to baptism at the hands of John, but the
symbolism of water and the dove adds far more. Christ
becomes one with rest of Salvation history. His baptism is
part of the long line begun with Creation. The Spirit
present at the first Creation is present at the inaugural of
the New Creation (2 Cor. 5.17). The turbulent waters of
Chaos yielded to the Spirit in Creation and subsided at the
presence of the dove sent out by Noah. The baptismal
waters in which Christ stood were, presumably, not
turbulent. To the evangelists, however, they represented
the Chaos yielding now at the presence of the Spirit and
the Anointed.

The Gospels May be Viewed as a Whole

As beautiful as any individual gospel may be, a single gospel (as a single sermon) cannot present the entire majesty of the personality of Christ. "There are many other things about Jesus; if all were written down, the world itself, I suppose, would not hold all the books that would have to be written." (Jn. 21:25). Some fine Christian scholars are so persuaded of the uniqueness of the Evangel of John or Luke or one of the others, that they are reluctant to see their portraits mingled. Mindful of the above citation from John, Ignatius did not hesitate to use a portrait of Christ drawn from many sources. Nor shall we hesitate. Christians can agree on this: Christ is bigger even than the gospels!

Ignatius' Parable

Fr. Ignatius introduces a parable at this point and his parable has proved a stumbling block for many. There are two reasons for this. First of all, the main example in his parable is archaic; it refers to a world other than the one we know. This problem is solved; we can translate the parable into modern terms. The second problem is a bit more difficult. Most readers of the *Exercises* approach the parable with excessive literalness and do not understand what Ignatius intends. We shall return to this problem after translating the parable:

The Summons of the Candidate

"Imagine to yourself a viable candidate for the Presidency of the United States. He presents himself to you and says, 'This is my program. On attaining the Presidency, I shall devote the resources of this great nation to eliminating all natural ills. We shall wipe out disease and hunger among men. In redistributing the wealth of the world, we shall eliminate all reason for world conflict. We shall eliminate ignorance and fear. In the climate that shall result, it will be easy for us to bring men to concentrate on the truths which revelation has to offer and to fix their gaze on a still better world than the one which you and I shall make for them.

"The path of my campaign will not be easy. You will have to leave home for some years as we follow the route of the primaries and bring my message to all men. You will suffer physical want during the campaign and be vilified for working with me.

"But this I can promise you. At the end, we shall prevail. As you have suffered with me in the campaign, so shall you enjoy with me the satisfaction of seeing ignorance, ill-health, fear and world-conflict disappear."

St. Ignatius asks, "what would our response be to such a summons? What sacrifice would we not make for such a candidate? Is there anything we could refuse him?"

Literalists that we all are, most of us respond badly to Ignatius' parable. We protest that there never was such a candidate and none is likely to appear. If he did appear and if he was what he protested himself to be, how could he possibly guarantee us the victory?

Ignatius replies with some firmness that we must allow our imaginations to wander here, to overcome our preoccupation with harsh reality. How *would* we respond? What *would* we offer such a candidate if he did exist? Only when we admit the depth of the emotions so tapped, does Ignatius go a step further.

The Candidate is Jesus Christ

The parable is but a symbol. The campaign, the goals, the guaranteed victory are images of the Call of Christ. Ignatius of course, was a Romantic and most lack the courage to follow our Romantic nature. Could this be one reason why he was so much more successful in the real world than the rest of us are? Ignatius will continue to make demands on our imagination. In his "gospel contemplations," he will insist that we enter into the scene described, that we hear the words uttered, that we see the actions take place. (And that we conclude our gospel contemplations by "conversations" with Christ).

Is all this some kind of game or does it have a foundation in reality? Actually, there is a dual reality here, theological and psychological. The theologian would observe that all things are present to God. Time and space may be problems for us, but not for him. The strength of the gospel accounts are eternal and without spatial limits. The psychologist would say something else. If we cannot enter into a given gospel scene, but enter easily into others, if we can only hear the words and see the persons in certain limited gospel stories, then some "psychological blocks" are afoot. When we cannot see and cannot hear, what are we to do then? Ignatius would certainly urge us to speak to Christ "as one friend speaks to another," asking him to explain to us the nature of the block so that by understanding it we may come to break through it and thus more deeply to hear and see and taste the fullness of the gospel message.

V

"AND THE WORD WAS MADE FLESH" (Jn. 1:14)

Ignatius was an insightful psychologist. He had lived for some years a rather un-Christian life, but came to lead one of utter dedication to the Gospel. Through introspection he then grew to understand the human process assisting the leading of the Lord who brought about the change in Ignatius' life. Once Ignatius understood this process, he was in a position to help others to bring similar changes (with the grace of the Divinity) into their own lives.

Ignatius speaks frequently of asking for the gift of "deep interior knowledge" as a means of bringing about desired changes. Here he refers to the two kinds of knowledge that Newman came to call "real" and "notional." As a simple example of the latter, many Americans are vaguely aware that smoking, over-eating, lack of exercise are detrimental to their health, but the knowledge is not "real" and has little motivating effect on the way they live. So most Christians have a "notional" knowledge of what the Incarnation means, but until the knowledge becomes real, it cannot be a driving force in their lives. And, in the matter of the Incarnation, knowledge does not easily become real, even for the gifted theologian.

This is easily proved. Some years ago, there was offered by medical researchers an explanation of the issue of blood and water from the side of Christ (Jn. 19:34) (in the hypothesis that this was stark narrative without heightened symbolism). The researchers concluded that such an issue was easily explained if Jesus suffered from a congenital heart defect. One theologian wrote immediately that such an explanation would be "unacceptable to theologians." Why so? One may wonder if there is not implicit in the above objection a somewhat faint-hearted acceptance of the Incarnation: Jesus became truly *human*. To be human is to have weaknesses, physical and psychological. If Jesus is "like us in all things, sin alone excepted" (Heb. 4:15), then he shared these weaknesses. This is no proof that Christ suffered from any particular weakness (to be human is to have weaknesses and strengths), but immediately to reject the possibility of physical weakness in Jesus is to lack real knowledge of what the Incarnation means.

Jesus is truly God and truly Man. The mainstream of Christian tradition insists that both of these statements are true. The history of the Christian Church is filled with a variety of errors flowing from the difficulty of accepting both these propositions. Men have tended to insist that Christ was not really divine, but only seemed so, or was somehow semi-divine, that he was not really human, but only apparently so, or some strange mixture of the human and the divine. Christ is truly human and truly divine. This is the Christian message. Ignatius, Christian, psychologist, and master of the Spiritual life, insists that we must accept both of these propositions and that our acceptance of them must involve a real knowledge of what they entail. Only thus will we be properly motivated to lead a life based on the fullness of the gospel teaching.

"And they went down to . . . Bethlehem" (Lk. 2:4)

Ignatius in writing of the account of the Nativity makes a delightful slip. Here his cultural conditioning overcomes the force of the usual charismatic insight. "We are to see here the Virgin riding on a donkey, accompanied by St. Joseph and attended—it may be piously thought—by a single maid-servant." Many traditions of Ignatius' time gave some support to the picture of the donkey (although its presence is most unlikely) and absolutely no support to the presence of the servant girl. Ignatius was conscious of this latter and covered his scholarly scruples by adding the phrase "as may be piously thought." One is reminded of the suburban moppet who wrote an essay about a poor family: "The father was poor; the mother was poor; the maid was very poor!" As a Basque nobleman, Ignatius could not bring himself to believe that Joseph and Mary were so poor as not to have one single servant in attendance. But they were.

The journey to Bethlehem, in the mind of Luke, took place on foot. Certainly we are appalled at the prospect of such a journey being made on foot by a pregnant woman. Our shock rests in a dual lack of understanding. We do not understand the nature of poverty in the ancient near east. Nor do we understand the sturdiness of the Palestinian peasant. Such were Joseph, Mary—and Jesus—sturdy Palestinian peasants. Generations of living close to the soil in a hard land had given them a toughness we may find hard to grasp. This is not to say that they did not feel discomfort and suffering. Rather they had come to accept a high measure of discomfort and pain as a part of life and did not struggle uselessly against it.

One may sometimes read nowadays that Jesus' life cannot be used as an argument to support a life of *asceticism,* the voluntrary embracing of the difficult and uncomfortable as a means of greater union with the

Divinity. Certainly we have gospel evidence that Jesus enjoyed "the good things of life." (This too is truly human). But to see the life of Jesus as non-ascetic is to ignore the discomfort of Palestinian peasant life, long before Jesus' passion and painful death, and to ignore the Christian tradition that this life was chosen willingly, of all possible lives.

Jesus and the Anawim

Although Luke wrote largely for a non-Jewish audience, the strong Jewish note of the apostolic preaching rests at the core of his message. In the account of the Nativity, he seems not to stress physical discomfort (which his audience would take for granted) but something else. Joseph and Mary make their move because "a decree went out from Caesar Augustus" (Lk. 2:1). An Old Testament motif is clear here immediately. The Old Testament speaks regularly of the poor (*anawim*). What it stresses is not their lack of material goods but their lack of independence. They are the pawns of forces beyond their control in a society which is steadily becoming more complicated. The *anawim* in the Old Testament come vaguely to recognize their helplessness: they have no recourse but to cast themselves on the Lord. They do just that. The New Testament adds only that the *anawim* are to be the privileged citizens of the Kingdom of Heaven. These are the "poor in spirit" praised in the Beatitudes and promised rewards (Mt. 5:3-12; Lk. 6:20-23). The wealthy, the learned, and the powerful are not excluded from the kingdom. No one is excluded. But it is the *anawim* who inherit the kingdom as their own.

The Genealogy of Jesus

The genealogies of Jesus vary in the gospel accounts.
(Mt. 1:2-17; Lk. 3:23-38). One begins with Abraham; the
other with Jesus and ends with Adam. The listings of
names are mysterious; they are found in lists of seven or
double sevens, the mysterious perfect number of the Old
Testament world. The genealogies stress a number of
things. Jesus does not come out of nowhere. He may be
the center of salvation history, but he does not begin it.
The legitimacy of Jesus as heir to David is also stressed.

But unmistakable is the stress on the humanity of Jesus.
Matthew, for example, cites four women in the genealogy:
Tamar, Rahab, Ruth and Bathsheba. What is their common
denominator? Possibly there is none, of course. The
involutions of scriptural composition are frequently lost to
us. On the other hand, we must be careful to avoid reading
in structures of our own. Many commmentators suggest
that the common denominator is that the four are
foreigners, non-Jews, and that the stress here is that Jesus
belongs to all men; his ancestry flows not from Jewish
blood alone. There may be another common denominator.
Tamar (Gn. 38:18), Rahab (Jos. 2:1), and Bathsheba (2
Sam. 12:24) enter the genealogy via incest, prostitution
and adultery. Ruth may have believed herself to be
engaging in the marriage act (Ruth 3:7), but many other
ages would view the act as fornication. So one message of
the genealogy may be that the Divinity can use everything
to shape his ends—even human weakness. God eventually
became flesh. At least the remote ancestry of the Incarnate
Word reflects the weakness of that flesh.

The House of Bread

"And they went down to David's Bethlehem" (Lk. 2:4), so called to distinguish it from other towns of the same name. *Bet lehem*, in Hebrew, is a fairly common name for ancient Canaanite towns. Its original meaning was probably "temple of *lhm*," the god of grain and consequently bread, the food-staple of the ancient world. Is it impossible to see here an allusion to the "bread of life," a motif which comes to us through other traditions? (Jn. 6:1-71; Mk. 6:30-56). Men have always feared physical hunger. In ages in which that hunger is assuaged, men become conscious of another pressing hunger. This will Jesus satisfy. It is seemly that Jesus should be born in the city of *Bet lehem*.

The Magi

Some may feel that the magi have suffered badly in recent biblical scholarship. To be sure, there was a brief period when they were dismissed as "only a *midrash*." (The *midrash* is a Jewish literary device, an embellishment of a story to teach a lesson). Later study by biblical scholars discovered that generally a *midrash* does not arise out of nothing. These mysterious personages, then, may have had some historical foundation.

In any event, the Evangelist uses the magi to teach a lesson. Perhaps the lesson in our time has best been grasped by a non-professional student of the Bible, Evelyn Waugh, whose literary sensitivities led him here to the heart of the Matthaean teaching.

In his novel *Helena*, he shows this great lady in her old

age, meditating drowsily in the Holy Sepulchre Basilica on the feast of the Epiphany. She sees the "wise men" as rather foolish, bringing unnecessary gifts which were "accepted and carefully put by as they were brought with love." She sees them taking careful calculations to journey properly, where the shepherds (the *anawim*) ran happily barefoot. She sees the magi then as the forerunners of many, many later Christians, who will come to Christ not easily as the little people do, but who will be welcomed there nonetheless:

"Dear Cousins, pray for me . . . for his sake who did not reject your curious gifts; pray always for all the learned, the delicate, the oblique. Let them not be quite forgotten at the Throne of God when the simple come into their kingdom."

Perhaps it is easier for the simple to accept the fact that Jesus is truly God and truly man. They do not ask for a reconciliation of this double statement, but allow it simply to change their lives.

One is apprehensive about excessive sentimentality in this meditation. Can it be avoided? The sight of the Eternal Word, Incarnate as a helpless infant, admits of sentimentalizing, certainly. Here Ignatius' restraint in writing serves him well:

"We enter the Cave and observe the scene, look at the infant and hear the persons speaking. We note the poverty and discomfort of the setting and reflect that the Divinity is here present. Before Him then we bow down and adore."

VI

"IS THIS NOT THE CARPENTER'S SON? ... "
(Mt. 13:55)

The New Testament, of course, is a complicated composition. The gospels especially are far more delicate and textured in structure than they appear to the casual reader. They are built in layers. While the isolation of these layers, the one from the other, is the work of scholars, an occasional adversion to their existence can be illuminating for the man of faith. The last uniting feature of the gospels was their formulation into proclamation—the preached instruction of the early church. The church took previous formulations, composed most certainly of the words of Jesus of Nazareth and reflected on them. Words, even events, flowed into the gospels which the original witnesses had not understood. (Mt. 3:15, Jn. 13:7). The gospels then are a Spirit-guided amalgam of reflection and word and work.

In this scene in Matthew, we have one very real component at the base. Hearing the Lord preach, tasting the wisdom in his words, the synagogue folk were very puzzled and one of them blurted out what was on everybody's mind: How is it possible for this man so to conduct himself? Is he not the carpenter's son? We all know him and his people, his mother Mary and his relatives James and Joseph, Simon and Jude. They are folk like us. Where did this wisdom come from?

The question of this fellow townsman of the Lord was heard by many and treasured by the early church. Why?

Because it summed up one of the great mysteries of Christianity in the life that the Lord lived and left to us as an example. "Is this not the carpenter's son? Whence this wisdom?" How can he preach so? How is it that he touches all hearts? We know him and his people. He is a *carpenter*.

Nothing had betrayed him. All those years of hard work (but no harder than that of all the peasants around him) were truly a hidden life. So hidden that when the Divinity revealed itself, those around were not ready.

Ignatius reminds the exercitant regularly during this phase of the exercises that he is to observe (and to wonder at) the manner "in which the Divinity conceals itself." It should be remembered that the goal of the exercises is primarily not the making of a decision, but coming into such union with Christ that the proper decision may be gracefully made. It might be proper here to stop and reflect on what manner of person he is. He lives for thirty years in a small Palestinian village, so like all his countrymen, so devoid of any spectacularly different characteristics, that one wise sermon is enough to dumbfound his fellows: where did this wisdom come from?

The principal role of this meditation, as always, is concern with the person of Jesus. If the spirit so moves us, we might stop right here and discuss the simple question with the Divinity: Is this not the carpenter's son . . . ? What is it to do the will of the Lord?

For those whom the Spirit does not call immediately to such prayer, there is another observation. The Divinity does not need anything. Even the actions of his only begotten son are not measured in terms of achievement. Certainly the Christian message—that striving rather than doing is demanded of us—lies at the heart of this mystery.

How necessary is this message for so many Christians for such long periods of their lives! The sick, the psychologically and physically handicapped, the untalented, the talented without opportunity, the talented who are circumscribed by the demands made on them by others: parents, spouses, children. To those whose talents have not developed due to circumstances beyond their control the gospel says: it is not achievement but striving that is demanded of you. "Is this not the carpenter's son?"

> *"And He went down to Nazareth and was*
> *subject to them. . ." Lk. 2:51)*

The Gospel of Luke (2:41-51) tells us here much the same story. The manner in which the Divinity conceals itself in this passage is sometimes lost. The narrative tells of a momentary departure from the ordinary, when the child Jesus slips away from Joseph and Mary to spend some days in the temple, putting questions to the temple scholars who wonder at his gifts. Certainly the child revealed himself as a bright young boy. We have little reason though to suppose (as imaginative later traditions embellish the tale) that Jesus was eager and brilliant in his "refutation" of Temple positions. There was little that he would wish to refute; most of the contemporary Temple *dogma* (as opposed, perhaps to a few of its practices) became part of his teaching. No, the image of Jesus as a youthful inquisitor does not flow from the gospel passage. What does come forth easily is the image of the hero, even from childhood, showing an occasional flash of what is to be. This image, the child as teacher, the church preserved for us.

But there is more to the story than this: My child, why have you done this to us? See how worried your father and I have been in looking for you? (2:48-49); and the child's mysterious reply to the loving couple: Did you not know that I must be busy with my Father's affairs?

And his mother stored up all these things in her heart (2:51). She accepted the child's mysterious explanation and took him back home with her. She was learning a vital Christian message: *to know the will of God is not always to understand it.*

"And Jesus grew. . ."(2:52). For those of us who are deeply convinced of the Divinity of the Incarnate Word, the force of this sentence is sometimes lost. He grew; he changed; he learned; he made human mistakes. Writings of modern theologians on the notion of the emerging messianic consciousness of Christ are not always clear. What is clear is an idea seen as early as Cyril of Alexandria. The Jesus of Nazareth who learns as we do, who learns by groping, who must apparently, as we shall later see, agonize over religious decisions, this is a Jesus with whom today's Christian can identify most easily. "And Jesus grew in wisdom, age and favor before God and men" (2:52).

It was in terms of the above scriptural allusions to the "hidden" life that Cardinal Newman coined his happy phrase describing the role of the saint whom the church called Confessor ("Proclaimer of the Christian Message"). He compared their lives with the dramatic pain of the Martyr and the spectacular brilliance of the Doctor and concluded that its essence was "weary perseverance in well-doing." This, of course, is the message of the hidden life. That Jesus so persevered in the humdrum that a single thoughtful sermon was enough to provoke the reaction cited at the beginning of our essay.

"Waiting for the consolation of Israel . . ." (Lk. 2:22 ff) It is not a distraction from the person of the Lord to look at those around him in the gospel proclamation. The gospels show us the Lord in many ways. One of them is the Lord reflected in the reactions of those whose lives touched his.

In fulfillment of Hebrew law, the infant Jesus is presented in the Temple. The child is offered to God and then redeemed—or "bought back"—with the offering of the poor. It is on the occasion of the presentation that there is some contact between the child Jesus and "a man named Simeon" (Lk. 2:25). The gospel of Luke tells us that Simeon had been specially taught by the Spirit. He had been assured that he would not die until he had looked on the *messiah*, the anointed of Israel, chosen by the Divinity for a variety of precious tasks. He is "prompted by the Spirit to come to the Temple" (27). Coming into contact with the infant, somehow, he takes him into his arms. Moved by emotion, he spontaneously composes a poem—as Semites are wont to do. Luke's gospel conveys it in the following words:

> *Now, Master, you can let your servant go in peace*
> *just as you promised,*
> *because my eyes have seen the salvation*
> *which you have prepared for all nations to see,*
> *a light to enlighten the nations*
> *and the glory of your people Israel (29-32)*

The prophecy was not a moment of unmitigated joy for the man. He saw that the work of the child would be to some extent rejected (34). Moreover, he may have seen that the Virgin would agonize with him (35). But for the moment we shall dwell on one other aspect of this vignette. We do not know that Simeon is old.

Christian tradition tends so to portray him, praying that his life may end now, that anything further would be anti-climactic now that his life's goal is attained. But we may ask the question: where did Simeon come from? Where did he go after this experience? As so often, the gospel presents us here with a frozen, knife-edge moment from a man's life. We are left then to speculate on what the rest of it was like.

As was suggested in our opening parable, the man who leads the life of Christian faith may expect long periods where he experiences little apparent contact with the Divinity. It is, however, the normal experience of the life spent in seeking Christ, that the Christian finds (as did Simeon) the moment of contact capable of blotting out the memory of the years that preceded and of coloring all the years that may follow.

Here we may follow the standard advice of Fr. Ignatius and imagine ourselves to be participants in these events, to see ourselves as part of the synagogue crowd, to mingle with those in the Temple, to hear Simeon's voice. Then most important, having attempted to share the experiences of these gospel figures, we are to speak with the Lord and to express ourselves openly. It may seem to us, especially in the beginning, that our "conversations" with the Lord do not make a great deal of sense. We do not say the right things and we do not hear what it is that he is saying. But this really does not make very much difference. "The Spirit helps us in our weakness, for we do not know how to pray as we ought, but the Spirit himself intercedes for us with sighs too deep for words" (Rom. 8:26).

VII

A CONTEMPLATION ON CHOICE

Ignatius was a masterful psychologist. But, of course, his knowledge of psychology was limited by those psyches with whom he came in contact. It is a commonplace to note that Freud's work must occasionally be separated from the common psychological distress of turn-of-the-century Vienna in which it originated. Perhaps the need to do something similar for Fr. Ignatius is no place clearer than in his treatment of Hell and Satan. Ignatius was thinking of a psyche somewhat different from that possessed by most of us who now devote some time to the great themes of the Exercises. Many of those persons for whom he shaped the Exercises had not devoted a moment since the age of twelve to anything approximating "spiritual activity." This was understandable in a society which, in some measure, threatened always to reduce such activity to the world of children. Ignatius moved boldly—almost harshly—in an effective move to get such a person's attention.

His treatment of the topic of Hell and the personal sins of one's own past life are quite blunt—as shall be seen in part II of this book. Our treatment of these topics must be a bit different. This is so, because we must be true to Fr. Ignatius' first principle: that goods are to be used in so far as they are useful to us in enabling us to draw closer to the Divine Majesty. Therefore, we approach these topics in a manner that will enable the readers (and contemplators) of this book to attain the goals that Ignatius had in mind for his exercitants.

We put a rather positive stress on our approach to a contemplation on personal sin. So too the externals of our approach may seem to differ from the externals of Ignatius' approach in another major topic of the *Exercises.*

Hell

Fidelity to the heart of Fr. Ignatius' technique will compel us to present one of his ideas differently. His language, derived from portions of scripture, from Church documents, and from the pious commentaries on both, written in his own day, seems a bit preoccupied with Hell as a place of enormous physical distress. Ignatius, of course, was faced with a problem of descriptions. Certainly the thrust of Christian teaching insists on the theoretical possibility that man can offend God absolutely and die unrepentant. (Neither scripture nor Church documents, however, have ever cited someone who did). Should this happen such a person would be eternally in *a place where God's love is not*; and this is Hell. It is not always easy for us to grasp the terrible pain of being in *a place where God's love is not.* For those moments, perhaps, the imagery of fire might be of some use if it does not distract us from the image of a Christ that loves. Remember that Ignatius in his own treatment of Hell notes that it is to provide motivation that may keep us from future sin "if we should become forgetful of God's loving care." We may then reflect on Hell in any manner we wish, provided that we stop frequently to repeat as an antiphon, an amplification of John 3:16 found in the Roman Ritual: "God so loved the world that he gave his only begotten son and the son so loved us that he gave himself for our salvation." If we repeat that antiphon often enough and listen to the voice of the Spirit in the silence that follows it, we shall be led doubtless by the Divinity to a fuller understanding of the role of Hell in the divine plan.

Satan, Chaos, Myth

At this juncture, Ignatius suggests some moments of reflection on Satan—and that suggestion is puzzling enough. Are we being asked to make a *choice* between Christ and Satan? (Ignatius' meditation could easily be called a contemplation of Choice). No, that cannot be. We shall return to this in a moment, but first, who is Satan for the modern Christian? Remember that this work purports to be a work of sturdy piety.

Much needless excitement is stirred up in the hearts of some Christians when they hear the word *myth*. Like some of Ignatius' early adversaries, they do not stop to ask their fellow Christian "what he meant by his idea" or "is there a benign interpretation which I can place on it?" Myth is not a word to be feared. It is the use of poetic language to recapture a reality that simply cannot be recaptured in any other fashion. What "literary form" would be most useful to a young man in love as he tried to represent on paper the experience of seeing his beloved smile at him for the first time? Now we generally think of anatomical language as being precise and accurate. And it is—within limits. If the young man had had a good first year course in human anatomy, he could detail all the muscles involved in moving the facial structure so as to reveal the bone-structure (the teeth) protruding from the gum tissue of his beloved's mouth. But would this really recapture the moment? Of course not. Therefore the young man would have recourse to images of roses and snow and feelings of light and warmth because they could describe his beloved's smile. And the anatomical description simply could not.

There are powerful realities lying behind the message of the Scriptures, Old Testament perhaps a bit more than New, that found their most effective expression in mythic language. Both Testaments, for example, grappled with the problem of an adversary with whom God contended. Neither Testament made the mistake of the pre-Hebraic literature of seeing the "adversary" as the equal of God in the struggle. Still, the New Testament with the mention of Satan thirty times and *devil(s)* nearly a hundred, the Old Testament with references (sometimes veiled) to chaos, forces of darkness, and the dragon, are using mythic language to teach a complicated truth. We would be unfaithful to this language were we to attempt to translate it into more direct statements.

We need not. Suffice it to say that Ignatius is on excellent ground when he urges the exercitant to imagine the existence of Satan, the type of person he is, what his cohorts are like, the territory that he inhabits. And then to reflect on the person of Christ. Briefly put, all that Christ is, Satan is not. We are, however, to devote much time to seeing just that, at least with the vision of imagination. Why so?

It is, of course, clear that Ignatius could not be urging on us a simple choice between good and evil. That choice is long since made or we would not be praying the exercises. Rather, Ignatius is trying to show us the possible totality of the decision for Christ. We are not opting simply to do good things, but to become good persons, with a special kind of goodness, growing steadily into the image and likeness of Christ.

Therefore, Ignatius suggests that we allow our imaginations a loose rein here, pretending to ourselves what is evil and associating it with Satan, imagining all that is good and associating it with Christ. It is a total reorientation of our life that is sought and we must be aware of the totality of the decision.

Ignatius suggests that this meditation end with "conversations" with God the Father and God the Son, that we ask them for an understanding of the fullness of the Christian message and for the courage to accept the consequences of that understanding. Each of these conversations is to be followed by the slow recital of the Our Father as we prepare for re-entry into a workaday world, confident that the Spirit will follow us into that world to interpret for us the message of the Father and the Son.

VIII

DEGREES OF COMMITMENT

Ignatius presents something for reflection at this juncture that might be expressed in the following bizarre little parable.

"There were once three men who had excellent health habits—with one exception; they would begin each day with an eight-ounce glass of carrot juice. (And we all know how unhealthful *that* is). On a given day, each was given a thorough medical examination and each was told by his doctor: "In the light of the best medical knowledge available, we now know that carrot juice is very unhealthful. You really ought to give it up."

Each man had a different reaction. The first one said: "Doctors, what do they know?" and he ignored the advice. The second man said, "I am certainly concerned for my health, but carrot juice tastes so good in the morning... I think I shall start walking vigorously forty-five minutes a day. Everyone knows that is good for one's health."

And the third man said: "That is it. I shall never drink a drop of carrot juice for the rest of my days." And he never touched it again.

The example "carrot juice" was chosen, of course, because so far as is known, it has never stood between anyone and sanctity. What it is that stands between a given exercitant and holiness is not for a director to suggest and certainly not for the author of a book. It is for the Spirit personally to teach. But Ignatius, who had a parable of his own, wanted the exercitant to reflect a bit on three ways in which men can respond. He once wrote, "As a general rule, the more openly and generously a man offers himself to the will of the Divinity, the more gracefully will the Divinity reveal Himself to him."

But a very important caution must be noted here. Certainly the Christian who wishes to grow into the likeness of Christ must have ambition to refuse God nothing that he clearly asks. *But we must insist that He ask clearly.* This is for two reasons. The Spirit will not underwrite ambitious spiritual projects which were not his idea. Persons who take on such projects will find with the passage of the years, months, (possibly even days!) that they are not up to the tasks; they grow discouraged. This one serious mistake accounts for a very large number of spiritual drop-outs. Secondly there is a law of elementary psychology afoot here. We know, of course, that God does not *need* anything from us. Still, He seems to encourage us to carry on a relationship that – while it is not one of the remotest equality – is one of friendship. Who of us has not seen friendships rent because one friend thrust on the other all manner of gifts and favors that the other had never sought or wished. And then the first friend refused the second the only favor that he had ever sought. There is surely something analogous to this in our dealings with the Divinity. It is his role to decide what he wants and so to inform us. But as did the great figures who run through all Jewish religious literature, we must insist that the Divinity speak clearly. We shall not hearken to mumbling or muttering.

Christ Arrives on the Public Scene (Mt. 3.1-12, Mk. 1.1-8, Lk. 3.1-19)

The figure of John the Baptist proclaiming the coming of Christ is certainly worth reflection. As did Simeon, the Baptist refracts certain aspects of the holiness of Christ. Certain contemporaries of the Baptist thought that his sternness indicated a type of asceticism that was more bleak than that of Jesus and his associates (Mt. 9.14-17,Mk. 2.18-22, Lk. 5.33-39). And Jesus' reply does not really suggest otherwise. It is true that the harshness of his own lifestyle is mitigated by the gentle aspect of his teaching. When soldiers and tax-payers are frightened by his denunciations and ask "What must we do?," like any good teacher, John begins where these students are. He tells them: "Do not gouge! Do not extort!" (Lk. 3.14). Like all absolutely honest men, John meets – almost from the beginning – their common fate: not to be ignored. Before that fate leads to an inevitable conclusion, John sets the example for all Christians. In one last witness, rehearsed for us in the lines of the Gospel of John, 4.29-36, he stresses that the role of all Christians is to bring other men to Christ and then to fade out of the relationship. One verse (30) of this discourse sums it up in the beautiful English translation of the late Monsignor Knox: "He must grow more and more; I must grow less and less."

Christ in the Wilderness

In rich poetic language, the synoptic gospels tell us that Christ was "tempted by the devil" (Mk. 1.12-13, Lk. 4.13, Mt. 4.1-11). The language and imagery of these passages is certainly deliberately mysterious. We have here a classic confrontation of Good and Evil. That this confrontation takes place "in the desert" certainly heightens the mysterious drama. Yet in all the gospels, Christ is "led by the Spirit" to this confrontation. This is an echo of an Old Testament theme: Chaos/Satan may be almost ever-present, but always subservient to the Divinity. So Christ may be tempted by Satan, but the Spirit leads him to the trial and supports him triumphantly through it.

What was the nature of Christ's temptations? We do not know. The gospels present us with a stylized drama. Presumably the conflict thus acted out took place for Christ in the stern arena where most of us struggle: in the inner recesses of the mind. The details of that struggle are not recorded. Each generation of Christians has made its own conjectures, aided — and doubtless sometimes hindered — by contemporary preoccupations. Scholars of our own age see Christ as facing an agonizing identity crisis.

Certainly this would be in keeping with the insistence of theologians that Christ learned as we learn — gropingly. But if the inner movements of that struggle are closed to us (to be made available to us perhaps in conversations with Christ), the externals that the gospels stress are worth examination. Ignatius examined them and concluded that there is a universal method used by the forces of darkness in tempting men. All men are led first to the desire of excessive material prosperity, thence to the acquisition of honors, and finally to pride. Ignatius seems to use this last as a kind of clinical term meaning a spiritual near-death, a loss of all esteem for things spiritual and a lack of sensitivity to the spiritual dimension.

And so he tells us to ponder all these things, suggesting frankly that it is not power that corrupts, but money. And we may well wonder where that leaves us. Some may feel that this is not a problem for them, that life is a constant struggle for necessities. In which case, Ignatius might wonder out loud if the Spirit were to suggest that they be concerned then with their attitudes toward money. (And might we all wonder first how "necessities" are to be defined?)

This is a difficult juncture for the exercitant. It is most unlikely that we are all called to lives of heroic poverty like the saintly Dorothy Day. What is essential at this point of the *Exercises* is that we be mindful of suggestions already made: that we be open in conversation with the Lord on these topics, that we try to be ready to refuse him nothing that he clearly asks, that we have the courage to insist that he ask very clearly.

IX

LIKE UNTO CHRIST

Tolstoy once wrote, "All happy families are alike." By this he meant that the dynamic of the relationships of love which kept the family members inter-acting were the same in all these happy families. Obviously they differ considerably in a variety of external ways. Perhaps the dictum of Tolstoy would be phrased otherwise — though far less beautifully — by saying "All relationships of love have a great deal in common." One of the properties that such relationships always possess is the process by which members of a loving relationship become somehow like one another as the relationship goes on.

Who of us has not seen this in a happy marriage? The shy or churlish member of the union becomes confident or gracious with the passage of years, absorbing these qualities from the spouse. It is certainly true that we become like that which we love. Consequently, we must have some caution about what or whom we love. Moreover, in the case of loving relationships with persons, we must come to know the other person as well as possible. Only in this way can the full force of the dynamic take place. It is for this reason that Ignatius devotes so much time in the *Exercises* to the person of Christ. If we come to know Him — as the gospels present Him to us — we shall become truly like Him. But we must know Him. The gospels, of course, are not psychological biographies, in depth, of Christ, whatever else they are or are not. The gospels do provide slight clues to the composition of such a study. This composition we can and must provide for ourselves, under the guidance of the Spirit, if we are to know Christ so that we may gracefully grow into his image.

The Healing at Evening

(Mt. 8.16-17, Mk. 1.32-34, Lk. 4.40) These gospel texts present a very simple idea. Their common message might be presented thus: It was evening. They brought the sick to Jesus and he healed them. It is possible, at least in some of the accounts, that this simple line may be a part of the passage which precedes. If this is the case, the mention of evening may be intended by the evangelist to point out that the Sabbath was not violated by the persons who carried their sick friends to Jesus. Or the intention of the evangelists may have been somewhat different. It may have been intended to present a kind of psychological *vision* of Christ. In this, surely, the evangelists were summing up incidents that had been witnessed dozens of times. The day had ended. The cruel Palestinian heat had ceased. The dramatic cooling off had begun which takes place in parts of Palestine with the setting of the sun. And with this dramatic drop in temperature, friends of the sick, weary after the long day but strengthened now by the cool of the evening, bring their friends to Christ. What the witnesses of these events remembered afterward was not any dramatic healing that may have taken place. No, they were struck rather by the image of the quiet and gentle Christ who seemed a part of that mercifully cooling late afternoon. And this then the evangelists tried to convey in the simple passage: It was evening. They brought the sick to Jesus, and He healed them.

Here Ignatius would certainly tell us to see ourselves as part of the throng around Christ, to hear Him speak, to see the reactions of His hearers. Most of all, we are to look on the calm which radiates from Him. It is true that our growth into the image of Christ is limited by our temperaments, our bodies, and our psyches. Still, it is the witness of Christian history that if we contemplate this — or any other gospel-witnessed aspect of Christ — eventually our lives will be affected by the contemplation.

I Tell You That Up Is Down

(Mt. 5.1-12, Lk. 6.20-23) With the sermon on the constitution of the Kingdom, we come to the heart of the Christian message. No Christian can read these passages without embarrassment. Sundry exegetes have tried to offer escapes from these dicta, but they do not work. Basically, the burden of all these paradoxical injunctions is this: Christians, real Christians, cannot fit into this world easily. All that it teaches: about money, power over others, and the assertion of one's own will at all times, this they must reject. All that it scorns, they must esteem. All that it ignores, must be primary in their lives.

The beautiful cadences of the beatitudes are so familiar to us that we tend to hear them with an accompanying exegesis of our own. We hear the words but we do not hear the message. We tell ourselves that "spiritual poverty" is what matters, that one may have great wealth but be "spiritually detached from it" (then how easy simply to get rid of it!). No, the message of the beatitudes is so stunning that we do not hear it.

There is perhaps one device we may use as an entrance to the powerful message of the beatitudes. Let us imagine some beloved religious leader of our acquaintance taking the posture of a teacher before a congregation that has known him well for some time and then hear him deliver a paragraph something like this: My dear Friends, I tell you that Up is Down, that Night is Day, that Sickness is Health, that to have utterly nothing is to be truly prosperous. All you have heard before my preaching was only error. That X, properly understood, is non-X. If you understand this, you have understood everything.

Certainly, our reactions to such an address would be complicated. Our first concern would be to wonder if we had heard correctly; our second would be concern that a beloved leader had lost his senses.

These would be the reactions of any follower of Christ hearing this sermon for the first time. This is one argument against the sermon's having been delivered so starkly as the gospels present it. Rather is it likely that these passages are faithful witness of the church to the message of Christ that she had reflected on, having heard it in the preaching of his lifetime and having understood it through the teaching of the Spirit.

This makes it no less difficult to accept. To say that it is easy to accept is perhaps to suggest that we have not understood it.

John's gospel presents us with another striking and related dictum: If you love me, keep my commandments (Jn. 14.15). The full force of Christianity can sometimes be lost by making such a dictum too complicated — or too simple. What does it mean for us today? Certainly the detailed meaning of "my commandments" is not so clear today as in some other ages. The church in each age relives the experience of Christ's passion. Some ages have felt it through persecution. Others have felt it in the pain of rending heresies. Ours feels it in a special way: some things are not so clear as they were — or as we thought they were in the past. And among them, the applications of "my commandments." But if the detailed applications of all the injunctions of Christ are not clear, *some of them are very clear.* And the force of these must be felt somehow in our lives, or we cannot keep telling ourselves — or him — that we love him.

The paradoxes of the beatitudes must find some place in our lives. This is pellucid. And these beatitudes must be exercised in dealings with persons. "If you love your fellow-man, you have fulfilled all" (Rm. 13.8).

We must reflect on all this and not grow discouraged. Steady growth into the likeness of Christ is compatible with failures; it is not compatible with discouragement, which is utterly to be avoided. "This was why (the Messiah) took to himself descent from Abraham, becoming completely like his brothers so that he could be a compassionate and trustworthy high priest of God's religion, able to atone for human sins. He has himself been through temptation and able to help others who are tempted" (Hb. 2.16-18).

We are to discuss all this in conversation with Christ and then, slowly, to recite the Our Father.

X

SUFFERING

*"Sacrifice is usually difficult and irksome; only love can
make it easy, and perfect love can make it a joy."* (Roman
Ritual)

With this we begin what Ignatius considered the third
"week" of the Exercises — a consideration of the events of
the Passion and Death of the Lord Christ. Here Ignatius
would have us — above all — consider "how the Divinity
conceals itself." The significance of these events, of course,
requires that we grant the fact of human estrangement
from the Divinity and the need for "redemption." The
possibility of personal estrangement from the Divinity
presents no theological problem to anyone honest enough
to begin making the *Exercises.* Who of us is not aware of
past sin? Having violated the commands of an infinite God,
most of us are deeply aware of having stood personally
under judgment and having needed desperately a mediator
who could speak on our behalf to the Father. The mode of
redemption, the innermost relationship between the aton-
ing death of Christ and our becoming at one with the
Father, perhaps best remains a mystery in the praying of
the *Exercises,* separated from the earnest efforts of
theologians to make the mystery a bit more intelligible in
human terms. Even here we do not disparage their efforts.
Their conclusions, though, are not especially useful to us
in the knife-edged moment of our contemplation. We have
been estranged indeed from an infinite God. Christ has
provided us with access to the previously offended

Divinity. And the mode of his providing the access has been through suffering and death.

We would here, most of all, be sure that Christ is at the center of the *Exercises.* Still, we would make our subsequent following of the Lord more difficult if we did not admit the role that suffering plays in our own lives. Here, as so often in practicing Christianity, nuance is terribly important. Our primary intention in living as Christians cannot be simply that a living Christianity makes suffering more tolerable. Even if it did not, we would be eager to embrace the great truths of the Christian message. But in fact it does. The view of "religion" that Harvard psychiatrist Robert Coles once enunciated, that it was comforting under stress to go into Black churches in the South, to hear hymns and to sing with the people, to touch them, to listen to affective homilies on the word of God — this is not all that there is to Christianity, but we need not be ashamed that it is part of it. Indeed, Christianity is deeply comforting, especially in the darkest moments, if we believe that we are "making up what is lacking to the sufferings of Christ" (Col. 1.24). Whatever else this may have meant to the suffering Paul, one thing seems clear. He saw himself as *making present* the effect of the redemptive sufferings of Christ and thought it fitting that he should himself be suffering as he did so.

We may be encouraged to think of our own suffering while meditating on the passion, if for no other reason than this: *failure properly to come to terms with suffering in our own lives will make impossible real growth in Christianity.* Somewhat cynically perhaps, Somerset Maugham once wrote that adversity did not teach, that the gentlest and the best men he knew were successful men

and that the failures he knew were bitter persons. Ann
Morrow Lindbergh phrased it better: "I do not believe that
sheer suffering teaches. If suffering alone taught, all the
world would be wise, since everyone suffers. To suffering
must be added mourning, understanding, patience, love,
openness, and the willingness to remain vulnerable."

So did Christ suffer. If we would grow into his image,
we must read the gospels carefully to learn the mode of his
suffering. Certainly, we are to "see how the Divinity
conceals itself." We must also watch how the revealed
humanity copes with suffering and thus learn.

The Death of Lazarus

(Jn. 11.1-44) This passage serves as the introduction to
the passion in John's narrative. Coincidentally, it gives us a
portrait of Christ with friends who are suffering. The
gospel story may be slowly read aloud. In the following
silence we should be one with the crowd, watching their
reactions and sharing them, and hearing the words of
Christ. One verse perhaps needs some special attention. Jn.
11:35 tells us, "Jesus wept." It may well be, as write many
commentators, that the evangelist wishes to stress that
Christ saw the implications of what he was doing, that
with this action the events of the Passion would be
inevitably set into action. The Evangelist may have seen
Christ as weeping at human perfidy and blindness. Or there
may be something simpler afoot. Christ is in the presence
of those who bear the burden of an exquisite human
agony; bereavement. Christ sees the bereaved person in
pain — and he weeps. There is a type of hardy Christian
who does not care for this explanation. He admires the

stern Jesuit of James Joyce who took "cold showers and
wore fresh white linen," and loves Socrates' quizzical
humor in the face of death. He is slightly embarrassed by
any display of gentle emotion on the part of Christ. He
tells himself that Christ displayed emotion as a concession
to us. Not so. The Christ of all the gospels is a deeply
sensitive person who is capable of great emotion. The
Divinity concealing itself reveals not all possible temperaments but one only — and that one is capable of feeling
great pain and showing it.

Palm Sunday

(Mt. 21.1-9, Mk. 11.1-10, Lk. 19.29-48, Jn. 12.12-29)
Certainly there is something unique about the Palm
Sunday narratives as they are shown in each of these
accounts. John stresses the role of Christ the King.
Matthew stresses prophecies fulfilled and miracles worked.
Luke highlights Jerusalem's struggle and destruction. There
seems to be a certain irony though that is common to all
of them. Christ acts out, apparently, a prophecy that is
stressing the uniqueness of his Kingship, that he is a king
who is redolent of humility and abhors the normal royal
display of pomp. The irony is that Christ, who could have
asked his Father for the company of "many legions of
angels" excites this crowd by the feeble gestures of royalty
which he permits on this occasion — so eager were they to
see him as a certain kind of king.
　　Ignatius would have us "mingle with the crowd and
listen to them," he would have us look on the scene and
listen — in imagination — to the unrecorded reactions of
the disciples. Perhaps nowhere in our contemplations on

the New Testament is the crowd more instructive than this one. The New Testament is sometimes accused of being anti-Semitic, perhaps not always without foundation. Much of the New Testament was composed in a period when the early church and the synagogue were having a family quarrel; such quarrels can be rather acrid and they may have affected the church's memory. Frequently, though, one can read an anti-Semitism in the gospels that is not there. Here for example, while the crowd is presumably largely Jewish, any irony directed at them in the gospel narratives is not so directed because they are Jewish. One of the oldest and best commentators on Mark says that this crowd is dimly beginning to see that Christ "is not the messiah of their hopes." It is thus that the narratives view them. And has the Christian church never in her history forgotten to look at the Messiah as he is, and dreamed rather of a messiah in another image? And we in our own lives? Have we never attempted to thrust the messiah into our pattern? Have we attempted always to learn the nature of his pattern?

In any event, now is our opportunity. Having mingled with the crowd and listened to them, we take Christ to one side and speak with him, "as one friend speaks with another." We ask him then to explain to us the nature of his messiahship, that we may accept that understanding and let this new knowledge then change our lives.

And we close the contemplation by reciting —slowly—the *Anima Christi.*

XI

PRAYER, EUCHARIST, AND DEATH

Thomas Merton once wrote that the reason why people could not understand St. John of the Cross was that his language was so bold that they judged it to be hyperbole and deducted ninety percent. What was left was still true, of course, but it was only ten percent of the original. Certainly there are passages in the gospel that have met the same fate. When the gospels begin to speak about prayer, what figures do they use? "How should you pray? There was once a judge who despised common opinion and had no belief in God. He did just what he pleased. A widow came to him for help and he refused her a dozen times. Finally he gave her what she wanted because he said: 'If I do not, she will simply wear me out!' " (Lk. 18. 1-8). "A man came to his friend in the middle of the night and asked him for some food. His friend lived in a one-room house. His whole family had mats rolled out on the floor and were asleep. There was no way to get to the food without waking the family, so he asked the man to come back later. But the man outside made such a rumpus, that the friend said: 'He is going to wake the whole family anyway.' So he gave him the food" (Lk. 11.1-8).

We would not tell ourselves to pray that way. If Fr. Ignatius gave us the advice, we might hesitate, but it is clearly the message of God's living word. And the church adds only: How much more will the Heavenly Father give the Spirit to them that ask" (Lk. 11.13).

Sometimes, even in a retreat, we become convinced that

we are not "good at prayer." The answer, of course, is to pray that we may become "good at it." How are we to pray? For one answer which the gospels offer, re-read the above.

The Eucharist

In the eucharistic words which the synoptics record for us (Mt. 14.22-25, and Lk. 22.19-20) a great deal is presupposed that is not always immediately known by a modern English-speaking audience. Certainly, for Americans of all people, the idea that the eating of any meal is a semi-sacred occasion is something that is not readily grasped. The hurried meal, eating and running, are too much a part of our culture. Not so in the ancient world. Perhaps part of this is simply explained. The appearance of food on the table was always a bit of a miracle in ancient Palestine. Circumstances of climate and soil made an annual crop ever precarious. However the idea originated, the meal's sacredness was established early. Some scholars see in verses like Exodus 24.11 ("They ate and they drank in his presence,") a ritual conclusion to the acceptance of a covenant between God and Israel; the covenant was sealed with the eating of a meal.

The Passover meal which Christ ate with his disciples was a festive meal. Presumably there were on the table varieties of delicacies which were rarely eaten. So the choice of the eucharistic elements may be significant. To this day in Jerusalem at various seasons of the year the streets are mobbed with pious pilgrims. One segment of them, the Greek orthodox pilgrims who come largely from Cyprus, are not greeted enthusiastically by the local merchants. Most of these pilgrims are like Jesus' closest

companions: they are desparately poor. Their pilgrimage
costs them only the price of the meanest transportation;
they sleep in the streets. And, as one of them told the
author, "If we have to buy food, we buy only bread and
wine!"

Bread and wine are the food of the poor. Is it forcing
the symbolism to say that the eucharist is the food of the
spiritually poor, the weak, that in the eucharist we have no
banquet for heroes, but sustenance for the weakest of us?

An Anglican priest once wrote that, troubled with
doubts on the meaning of the Eucharist, he used to pray
before each mass that he "might do what the Lord wanted
me to do." What a beautiful prayer! Even without doubts
of conscience, who of us will not want to utter that prayer
before Eucharists in the future?

Approaching Death

The fear of death is nearly universal. There is so much
contemporary discussion of it that we are running the risk
of turning one more formerly taboo topic into consum-
mate boredom. The risk must be run, as we wish to
approach the subject from a new direction: fearing the fear
of death. This is particularly a problem for those who are
elderly and pious. They feel that if they were truly pious
they would not fear death. Yet, since they are honest and
they know that they fear death, they become concerned
that this fear indicates a lack of real spirituality. Even the
great psychiatrist Dr. Kübler-Ross is not helpful here.
After her book *Death and Dying*, she wrote that some
persons were possessed of such a "deep faith" that they
did not fear death. This can be phrased better perhaps.

There are saintly persons (whose emotional health lies well within normal limits) who fear heights, snakes, or water; there are saintly persons who have no such fears. There are persons rather limited in spiritual gifts who have such fears or do not. The origin of these fears lies outside the realm of "deep faith." It is only true that the fear of death differs from some other fears because it is so nearly universal. Even those few persons who seem to lack it may have some experience of it in the moments before death. In such moments, with disintegration impending, what was once man is now largely animal and all animals fear death.

Christ feared death

If our contemplation of the passion narratives does nothing else for us, it should convince us that there is no contradiction between being a devoted Christian and having some fear of death.

There is value to be found in contemplating either the Johannine account of the scene in the Garden of Gethsemane (18.1-11) or the synoptic accounts (Mt. 26.36-46, Mk. 14.32-42, Lk. 22.40-46). It is true that the Johannine Christ is the serene master of the situation. Much reflection by the later Church contemplating the ultimate victory of the Lord Christ is visible in this account. The synoptics perceive another aspect of the same reality. Christ is depressed and anxious. Certainly he had some clear knowledge of his impending death, a Roman execution at that, and he prays for deliverance if it be the Father's will. We have little problem in any of the Synoptic accounts of "seeing how the Divinity conceals itself."

Looking back over these few pages then, we make our

insistent prayer that the Spirit be given to us more fully.
With his aid, we listen to the Eucharistic words, we see
Christ agonize over impending death. And we speak to
him, "as one friend speaks to another from whom he has
received an enormous favor."

And when we are through speaking we recite—slowly—
the Our Father.

XII

"AND THEY LED HIM TO CAIPHAS . . .
TO HEROD . . . TO PILATE."

Remember what we have noted earlier, that it is not
always a distraction in gospel contemplations to look at
those around Christ. In the case of the devout gospel
personages, each of them reflects some aspect of Christ's
holiness. In the case of other persons in the gospels, they
serve as partial negative images when they refuse to accept
one aspect or another of the holiness that they confront.
In the various passion narratives, portraits of at least three
confrontations are given us: Christ before Caiphas, Herod
and Pilate. We move cautiously. In a brief essay, one
cannot touch on all the legitimate implications of these
confrontations as the gospels show them. We have some
extra-biblical evidence on Herod's person and much
extra-biblical evidence on the classes of persons which
Caiphas and Pilate represent. The gospels, presumably,
highlighted certain points as consonant with the theology
which they preached. So shall we too write from a very
limited viewpoint in offering reflections. It is only the
Spirit who is unfettered, here as always, teaching with the
aid of the gospel message or moving around it.

Caiphas and Pilate were not monsters but human beings. By the time of the gospel events, Herod's title to humanity was surely considered weakened by a long life of debauchery in which his role as absolute monarch enabled him to live out all his bizarre fantasies to their ultimate rule and his personal destruction. But in the case even of Herod, it is important to remember that he was not ever thus. It remains a human capacity to make oneself less than human.

Caiphas
(Mt. 26.57-66, Mk. 14.43-64, Lk. 22.66-71)

The gospels give us a brief picture of Caiphas and it is not a flattering one. Surely some of this reflects the later quarrel between synagogue and church. Still, Caiphas' role in the events of the passion would seem to have been less than heroic. For the purpose of this reflection though, we are going to ignore that largely and to suggest something else. Caiphas, like Simeon at the Presentation, does not come out of nowhere. He has a history, a Before and an After. From what fragmentary knowledge we have of him from extra-biblical evidence, it is true that his life was not totally exemplary. The dimension of relations between synagogue and state make the role of the high priest in this point in history a very political one. His father-in-law had been high priest before him and nepotism makes Christians understandably nervous.

But there is one thing about much of his life before the confrontation with Christ (and possibly after it) that must be understood. As a boy and a young man destined for priestly office, his life had been hedged around with great discipline and self-sacrifice. Granting that his was at least normal intelligence, the study of the law required of him long hours of concentration and hard work. Nor can we put this to one side and assure ourselves that his motivation was "worldly." It surely may have become so. Still, in his earlier years there were at this historical period other avenues of "success" open to him. No, we must conclude that, as with many persons, his motivations grew more complicated as he grew older. But it is not inconceivable that at the center of his complicated motivation there rested a genuine love of the Divinity. The human heart is a dark well. Human vision is limited.

It can be said of human genius that its vision is not sharper than that possessed by most of us, but rather that it sees with a wider-angled lens; that you and I seek solutions in limited, clearly defined places—and so do not discover them. The genius, however, gazes at a wide horizon and finds the solution that we have missed. Part of holiness consists of a wide-angle view in search for the will of the Divinity. The narrower that view gets, the less likelihood there is of our finding what we seek. Caiphas' view had gotten very narrow and he could not find the will of God incarnated before him.

So limited was his vision, so convinced was he that God's will and the Temple—and that very narrowly defined—were coextensive, that he looked no further. This stubborn man before him was threatening the will of God as Caiphas saw it. And Caiphas acted in accord with his limited vision.

Some similar remarks can be made about Pilate. But perhaps we had better pause a moment to handle an obvious objection. What does such a view of Caiphas do with human responsibility? Perhaps one of the most awesome powers of human responsibility is our ability to lessen our capacity for exercising it. Having begun imperceptibly to narrow our vision, we arrive one day at the juncture where we cannot see and do not know that we cannot see. We have learned to keep secrets from ourselves. We are then no longer culpable. Moral theologians would hasten to answer that we would be culpable insofar as we had foreseen our ability to weaken our vision. It is the experience of many, though, that the human ability to delude oneself is considerable and that most persons can delude themselves fairly easily beyond the point of culpability.

At least two conclusions follow. Christians must be cautious in the extreme in judging the culpability of the evil that other men do. Secondly, we must pray earnestly for personal clarity of vision. The Old Testament prays for deliverance from "hidden sin" (E.g., Ps. 19.12): the sin that I may have committed unwittingly. Certainly we are dealing here with one dimension of that sin: the sin that we commit through blindness that is at least no longer culpable. Let us pray not so much for simple forgiveness of the hidden sin, but for our knowledge of it, that we may ask the Divinity to blot it out.

Pilate
(Mt. 27.11-26, Mk. 15.2-15, Lk. 23.13-25,
Jn. 18.28-40, 19.1-16)

In the view of the Roman Empire's mightier officials Pilate was certainly a lower echelon official. What higher echelon officials want from lower echelon officials is not to hear from them. Pilate knew this. He also knew that he

did not want to make a decision against Christ—or for him.
One gospel text tells us that his wife, with the aid of a
dream, is upset at the confrontation (Mt. 27.19). Still, to
some readers, some of the gospel descriptions seem to have
Pilate deliberately inciting the crowd (as in Jn. 19.15,
"What? Shall I execute your *king*?"). With the crowd
sufficiently stirred up, Pilate then shrugs his shoulders.
There is no decision to be made. He cannot tolerate the
possibility of a riot. The man must die.

One final comment. The people cry out: (Mt. 27.25)
"His blood be on us and on our children." What this line
cannot possibly mean was underlined by Vatican II in a
restatement of the obvious: the line inflicts no guilt on any
living Jew. It is certainly possible that Matthew's gospel
meant for the people to cry out that they would take the
responsibility for the death. The idiom is used with that
meaning once in the Old Testament (2 Sam. 3.29). Still,
with the Jewishness of Matthew's gospel and with the New
Testament's love of irony and a kind of "pun," it is hard
not to see something else here too. One of the common
uses of blood in the Old Testament was for sacramental
sprinkling on the people as remission of sins. It is hard not
to see here a pun in which an enraged mob says one thing
while meaning another. "May we be redeemed too!"

Herod
(Lk. 23.8-12)

Herod may be treated more briefly. His problems and
manner in which Christ disappointed him are probably
quite different from our problems and any "disappoint-
ment" which we find in Christ. Herod was jaded. He
wanted another thrill. He wanted to see a miracle up close.

Jesus would not cooperate, so Herod made fun of him and sent him away.

All these episodes have at least one thing in common. *To encounter Christ is not always to know him.*

Having seen the Divinity conceal itself in all these encounters, we are to have a conversation with Christ. The Spirit may lead us to discuss many things. Perhaps, though, we ought specially to pray that it be given us often to encounter Christ—and having encountered him to recognize him.

Then we shall recite—slowly—the *Anima Christi.*

XIII

GREATER LOVE THAN THIS . . .
(Mt. 27.32-56, Mk. 15.21-41, Lk. 23.33-49, Jn. 19.12-37)

When it comes to a discussion of the crucifixion, no man's eloquence is equal to the task. The gospel texts themselves are stark and beautiful; the message that Christian tradition has woven from these texts is truly awesome. Here more than ever, the writer—and the reader—can only hope for generous intervention from the Spirit.

First there is the mystery of "redemption." We have earlier mentioned that we could not discuss it in depth, nor shall we here. One aspect of the mystery though must be pointed out. In recent years, Roman Catholic theologians and teachers have worked mightily to stress one point: that the Divinity *needs* nothing from us. This is such an important truth and so many Catholics of a few decades back have had such difficulty in grasping it, that we move cautiously in any area which touches on it. Still, it should be said that God's absolute independence from man does not remove the possible mystery of "the offended God." Here we do not stress with Cotton Mather the "anger" of that God in whose hands sinners are, but the reality of God as a *person*. A good person, a loving person, even a merciful person would have to be *offended* by abuse of widow and orphan, by fraud perpetrated on the poor, by cruel injustice done to those who cannot fight back. And God is such a good, merciful and loving person. And He is somehow offended.

But Christ bears away the offense. This is the first and greatest message of the Crucifixion, whatever else we learn from it. "Our God is reconciled," and Christ is the focus of the reconciliation.

This Day in Paradise

Luke's beautiful episode of the "good thief" is touching in many ways. Most of us, most of the time, see our salvation as something *happening,* as a becoming in which we are given something, lavishly and gratuitously by a loving God. So was the thief reconciled. In two of the gospel accounts (Mt. 27.44, Mk. 15.32) this thief too is described as participating in the mockery of Jesus. One can only be sympathetic with both thieves. They were suffering from the worst of all deaths, as the Old Testament sees death. What was to become a "sudden and unprovided" death in Christian tradition, a death in which we are found spiritually unprepared, was something simpler in the world of the Old Testament. The death that was "violent and unforeseeable," the death that came on a man before due season or from outside source—that was the death against which a man could legitimately complain. And so did both thieves. Luke then sees one of the thieves finally refraining from his mockery and addressing to Jesus the wisest possible prayer: Remember me.

And Jesus tells him: this day you will be with me in Paradise (Lk. 23.43).

On such an important subject as death, the New Testament presents a variety of theologies. One view represented here and elsewhere (2 Cor. 5.8; Phil. 1.19-26) sees the Christian as being united immediately with Christ on death and with no "waiting" for the Last Judgment. It is true that with death, categories of time do not make a great deal of sense. It is also true that this view of death was then largely interpreted in the language of Greek philosophy which was not altogether suited to the task. Still, if one wishes to think in purely biblical terms, the "immediate" union of the Christian with Christ seems very well founded.

"Why have you abandoned me?"
(Mt. 27.46; Mk. 15.34)

We have in this agonized cry, the depth of Christ's suffering. But it is no cry of despair. This is the opening line of Psalm 22 where the speaker complains mightily to the Lord of his distress but speaks confidently that the Lord will end it soon. In fact, one modern scripture scholar sees in the difficult Hebrew of this psalm a line that reads: "The Victor (a divine title) restores to life!" Whether this judgment is true or not, the psalm seen as a whole is redolent of confidence in a coming justification.

The presumption on the part of scholars is that Christ—as any pious contemporary Jew—knew the psalm by heart and recited Psalm 22 at this juncture.

Paredoken to pneuma

(Jn. 19.30) And John the Evangelist with a beautifully ambiguous line tells us that Christ dies. The Greek above means: "He handed over the spirit," which can mean, "he gave up the ghost; he died" or "he made us a gift of the Spirit," that very same Spirit which makes it possible for you and me to speak with Christ through these gospel contemplations.

It is accomplished

Also in Jn. 19.30 do we read the above. Christ proclaims that his work is done and he dies. The joyous exultation of that line cannot be missed. But perhaps one nuance of it may be lost. Certainly Christ died in perfect fulfillment of the Father's will. But even for Christ, the cause of his joy was not the perfection of his activity, but his recognition of the father's work in him. Few of us at the moment of death will have the consolation of knowing how well we performed. We may, though, ambition the grace of seeing how well the grace of God performed in us.

This is beautifully expressed in the Noble prize-winning novel: *Kristin Lavransdatter.* The central figure of the novel is on her death-bed, moving in and out of consciousness, one moment animal, the next moment human. She has one insightful flash that "God had held her fast in a covenant made for her without her knowledge by a love

poured out on her richly ... [and that this] love had
wrought in her like sunlight in the earth, had brought forth
increase which not even the hottest flames of fleshly love
nor its wildest bursts of wrath could lay waste wholly."
Perhaps we should pray right now for the grace of such a
death.

Pieta

"After great pain, a formal feeling comes—
the Nerves sit ceremonious like Tombs ...
This is the Hour of Lead."

—Emily Dickinson

Christian tradition sees the body of Christ now as taken
from the altar of the cross and placed in the virgin's arms.
The artistic versions of the *pieta* from Michelangelo's
classic to primitive German woodcarvings seem to be in
agreement on one insight: they portray the virgin as very
young. It is true that she probably was young, as Jewish
girls of the period married early. Still, one may wonder if
the artistic insight touches something else. Christ's knowledge of the purpose and grandeur of the Passion may well
have been complete as he utters: it is finished. There is
little scriptural foundation for granting any such insight to
the virgin. The youthful face of the virgin (younger than
that of Christ in some of these presentations!) may reflect
the puzzlement of the child. Whatever the virgin saw at this
moment, she saw only through faith. Touchingly, the
German carvings are often called: *Vesperbild,* "picture at
evening" with overtones of Sappho's lyric:

Evening brings all things home . . .
the child home to his mother.
Some may find this sentimental—and it may well be.
Some may feel that in certain areas of Christianity, the
role of the Virgin has been "exaggerated."Perhaps, but the
thrust of Christian tradition insists that she is "the Mother
of God." A greater honor we cannot give her; this honor
we cannot take away.

We discuss then all these ideas, or those which the Spirit
has illumined for us, with Christ and the Virgin. We listen
to them for some moments and then we recite, slowly, the
Anima Christi and the Hail Mary.

XIV

ARISE MY LOVE . . .

With the contemplation of the Resurrection, we are
instructed by Father Ignatius to ask for the gift of
experiencing "joy with the Risen Lord." Indeed that joy is
great. One measure of its greatness may be the sundry
ways in which the reality of the Resurrection is conveyed
to us by the New Testament.

If one contemplates the reality of the Resurrection long
enough, surely one develops a taste for one or the other of
the New Testament scenarios. It is hard not to find a special
beauty in John the Evangelist's twentieth chapter. It is an
almost perfect locus for the type of contemplation which
Ignatius would have us make (John 20. 11-18). The
reflection that the Evangelist had made on the Resurrection enabled him to write this passage as a work of poetry,
written in an allusive vein with echoes of the Old

Testament's beautiful *Song of Songs*. The *Song of Songs* is variously interpreted, but all interpretations agree on this: it is a collection of songs of love, expressed between two individuals, an individual and a group, or two groups. In our gospel passage, the Risen Lord confronts Mary Magdalene—who does not recognize him. (This is a common pattern in the Resurrection stories and a reminder to us that the Resurrection is not a mere resuscitation; the Jesus that awakes is not simply a Jesus restored to health, but a Jesus endowed now with a new life, the life which he will bestow on all subsequent sharers in his Ressurection.)

John touches on memories of the *Song of Songs* starting with the fact Mary *searches* (Sg. 3) for the beloved. The search takes place in a garden (Sg. 4.12, 6.2). Of course, one of the motifs of the Song is that the beloved is asleep (Sg. 2.7, 8.4). Mary peers to look in through the opening in the tomb as the lover peers through the window (Sg. 2.9). A leisurely reading of the Song over some days will doubtless reveal other parallels to the exercitant. He should bear in mind that in the Song there is fairly steady confusion or mingling of roles between lover and beloved or active loving person and recipient.

John's beautiful passage may be otherwise read of course. On a simpler level, there is a beautiful encounter between a badly confused Mary ("Just show me his body and I shall carry it away myself!") (15) and a loving Jesus, who, when he chooses to make himself known, does so simply in calling her by name, "Mary" (16).

But there are two powerful reasons which make the view attractive that John's passage was written or rewritten in conscious imitation of the Song. First, if one were to reduce the Song to a single theme it would be: Love is as strong as Death (Sg. 8.6). Christianity insists that what all previous legend dreamed about, Christ accomplished. So strong was the love between Father and Son and overflowing onto us that it overcame Chaos, personified now as Death, man's ancient enemy. Jesus crushed Death and returned to us bearing, among other things, the promise that we too would crush Death in Christ's strength.

There is one other theme in the Song:

> *Come then my love*
> *my beloved rise*
> *For see, winter is past*
> *the rains are over and gone*
> *Flowers appear on the land*
> *Glad songs burst forth*
> *and we hear the voice of the Dove (2.10-12)*

Again, a land of primitive agriculture, rejoicing as we have said, with the simple appearance of food on the table in a given meal, went somewhat ecstatic with the coming of Spring. The first movements of life in the ancient earth reminded them that the forces of darkness and Death, temporarily unleashed by the Divinity and taking command in Winter, were now chained.

In the event of the Resurrection, those wintry forces were put to rout, at least to this extent: The power of the Resurrection is ever available to us to drive those forces back whence they came. Most Christians have a moment in their lives, a point after which the Resurrection's power came to play the dominant role in their earthly lives. Having died with Christ, they do now indeed live with him

(Rm. 6.8). It is hard, too, not to see here an allusion to that Dove which we showed to be present at Creation and at Christ's baptism and to be present evermore in the gifts of the Spirit which Christ has won for all who die and rise with him.

It is rare in making a retreat that one does not experience at this juncture a deeper sharing in the fruits of the Resurrection and in the gifts of the Dove. May it be so in the reading of this book.

"And Jesus said to her, Do not keep clinging to me"(17)

In this verse, we find an allusion to the sweet sadness of the Resurrection for us at this juncture. While it certainly is true, as Paul so insists, that we do now lead the Resurrected life, we continue to lead it in a mode that is different from the mode of our leading it in the end of days. John shows us Mary as not understanding this. She would, in the moment of her ecstasy, keep clinging to Christ forever and escape from space and time. He reminds her gently that the moment for such transitions is not yet come, and he gives her a chore to do—a pious chore, a happy chore, but a chore nonetheless, and he interrupts her ecstasy.

This is one view of the Resurrection. Certainly there are others. In some of the gospel accounts, it is difficult not to see a certain level of "playfulness" in one appearance of Christ or another. Whether this represents the apparent mood of Christ in these appearances as the witnesses remembered him, or whether it is an overflow of the joyous intoxication which the early church transmitted from those days, it is difficult to say. Eventually, another mood sets in. Persons outside the church began to suggest that the event of the Resurrection had not taken place; then the church reacted understandably but grimly, in presenting an "Apologia," a somber argument that the Resurrection did indeed happen. Those layers of the New Testament narrative are not so useful to us now, confident of our belief in the Resurrection and desiring only to implement it in our lives.

We may wish at this point to make a *reprise* to our parable of the Candidate and to remember his promise that were we to suffer with him in the campaign, we would enjoy our share of the fruits of his inevitable victory. Depending on one's temperament, contemplation of the Resurrection may make our share of the Passion easier to bear.

One of the old children's catechisms used to tell us, quite correctly, that man was made body and soul in the image and likeness of God and then, just a trifle primly to add: "That likeness is chiefly in the soul." The Resurrection shouts: *the likeness is also in the body.*

Reflecting then on these or other thoughts, as the Spirit leads, we pray for a large measure of joy with the Risen Lord. We speak then with Christ, as with a friend who has won a magnificent victory.

And then we read slowly, but happily, aloud: Anima Christi.

Contemplatio Ad Amorem

It has been written that one definition of a good Christian is that he is a person who sees that it is the one love of God which warms him in the May sun and chills him in the March wind. In terms of precise theology, that definition is perhaps not adequate, but there is a valid dimension to it. One of the factors involved in being a Christian is the ability to see the relentless, ineluctable drive of God's love in our lives. Only after death, when we are "with the Lord" and share his vision shall we see this drive in all its force. Still, gifted with Spirit, we can occasionally make an effort in this life to see how that force has operated in us to the present. Properly done, this results in what Ignatius called a *Contemplatio Ad Amorem*, "a meditation to increase the love of God in us," or "a vision of grace."

Ignatius calls us to review the history of our lives and frankly wishes us to review that history in the light of one prejudice: *the love of God has pursued us relentlessly*. Earlier, Ignatius called on us to examine our consciences and to look at our past lives and inquire how we had served the Lord. We did so cursorily, with the founded fear that we might make ourselves the center of the *Exercises*. Now though, slowly and with deliberation, we look at the same material—our past lives—and search earnestly for a vision of how the Divinity has worked in us.

There is only one caution in this meditation: as we look at those past years, we must not lose the point of the meditation by brooding over what might have been. We are to reflect on *what in fact was*, with a view toward coming to an insight like that of Kristin Lavaransdatter, seeing that God's love indeed has wrought in us like sunlight in the darkest earth.

Here we allow our minds to wander, subject only to the occasional reining back to our central theme: God's relentless love. We examine all the reasons we have to be grateful to the Divinity, beginning with the gift of existence itself. We reflect also on the gifts which came into existence and grew with us, whatever these gifts may be: physical, intellectual, psychological. Whatever natural good there is in us now, we see that incipient in our earliest memories of the years after infancy, unfolding, becoming more and more what they were meant to be.

Yet, anyone who has perdured to this point in the *Exercises* certainly esteems one set of gifts over all others: the spiritual, the supernatural, the God-oriented. We reflect on those gifts and on their unfolding. We look back at the conditions under which they grew, in infancy, childhood, youth, middle, or perhaps even old age. Who of us has grown in the love of God without being touched by human love? What memories do we have of childhood (and childish?) happiness flowing from the things of the Spirit? Memories of church services (when they were not too long!), some precious moment with a nun, with a priest, with parents, when the love of God seemed very real. If it seems in harsher light that those occasions were sentimental, that the devotions—judged by a more mature subject—were basically anti-intellectual, do we not see even now that the Divinity reached us as we were then and brought us closer to Himself?

Those of us who are at least in middle age have memories of a liturgical life quite different from that of the present. If in many ways the liturgy is better now (and it is; the church too grows and grows), if we experienced moments of unrealistic fear in the ancient liturgy, did not its awesomeness teach us something of God's grandeur? If we understood not the language, did the solemn Latin cadences not speak to us? And do not some of those echoes reverberate in us to this day?

In all these years, we were surrounded by companions, friends, relatives. What memories do we have of the growing love of God which we imbibed from each of them? What memories do we have of having helped these persons too to grow in the love of the Divinity?

In all the realities of our life, Ignatius would question, could the eyes of faith not see a purpose? Were we vigorous and healthy? Did this not lead us to the Divinity? Have we been unwell? Can we not see the divine hand in this? Were we successful? Did not these successes give us the courage to try and to dare more for the love of God? Have we failed? Has not failure taught us (at least sometimes) to rely on the divine strength? Has it not taught us some share of compassion for the weaknesses in others? Have we been in pain? Has that not taught us how frail we ourselves are? Was the pain taken away? Did that not free us to grow in the Divine Love?

And we stop for a few moments. We allow ourselves to be awash with waves of wordless thought. And we simply yield and give ourselves to those waves.

And Ignatius then asks three questions:

What have I done for Christ?
What am I doing for Christ?
What ought I to do for Christ?

Again, we pause before we answer.

In any relationship of love, challenge calls for response. There comes a moment when the fact can be delayed no longer that "Love is shown by deeds rather than words." If someone would be so churlish as to point out (and perhaps only the author would be so churlish at this juncture) that Christ does not *need* anything from us, and so the comparison is not a good one, perhaps an easy but correct answer is at hand: *in no relationship of love does the lover see the beloved as needing him or his gifts.* In the happiest of human loving relationships, each member of the union sees the other as beyond him, in no need of his gifts, *but the lover has a need to bring those gifts.*

> What have I done for Christ?
> What am I doing for Christ?
> What ought I to do for Christ?

We began these exercises in an effort to find the will of God. It may well be that the Spirit in his kindness has taught us that will in letters writ large. Or it may not yet be so. Perhaps God has answered our prayer by saying, "Wait!" What then? How are we to find the will of God now? A very wise Anglican Archbishop once wrote that we might begin by doing the best possible thing that we could do in the next five minutes, for what that is he said, we generally know although the more distant good is hidden. We discuss then all these things with Christ. And then we conclude the meditation—and the Exercises—

with the *Anima Christi.*

Lord, when I get to preaching, it is most difficult for me to know what are the movements of Your Most Holy Spirit and what are my own meanderings. . .It matters not. You draw good out of both. Amen.

cf. *Aurora Dawn,*
Herman Wouk,
Simon & Schuster,
N.Y., 1947, p. 44

PART II

Anima Christi

Anima Christi, sanctifica me.
Corpus Christi, salva me.
Sanguis Christi, inebria me.
Aqua lateris Christi, lava me.
Passio Christi, conforta me.
O bone Jesu, exaudi me:
Intra vulnera tua absconde me:
Ne permittas me separari a te:
Ab hoste maligno defende me:
In hora mortis meae voca me:
Et jube me venire ad te,
Ut cum Sanctis tuis laudem te
In saecula saeculorum. Amen.

(Ignatius did not write this prayer. He seems to have been very fond of it though. The speaker in the prayer perhaps was enough of a theologian to see problems in addressing Christ as "soul" and "blood" and "body." These are not separate entities of course but are united to the one Divinity. Still, as persons in love reflect now on the beloved's eyes or face or form without thinking of these as having a life of their own, so did the speaker of this poem.

The "translation" that follows must not be understood as an effort to reproduce in English the special beauty of the above. It is intended to aid anyone with a year of dormant high school Latin to be able then to read the above "in the original.")

Soul of Christ, sanctify me
Body of Christ, save (redeem me) me
Blood of Christ, intoxicate me
Water from the side of Christ, wash me
Passion of Christ, strengthen me
O good Jesus, hear me.
In your wounds, hide me
Never permit me to be separated from you.
From the evil foe, defend me
In the hour of death call me
And order me to come to you
That with your saints, I may praise you
For ever and ever. Amen.

A Presupposition*

"When one Christian suggests something to another, the recipient of the suggestion ought to accept the idea with one presupposition: that good Christians do not regularly make heretical and dangerous suggestions to one another! If the idea seems so, perhaps the recipient should ask himself: how did my fellow Christian intend the suggestion

*Throughout Part II, parentheses set off only Fr. Sheehan's personal remarks. All material not in parentheses is an effort to reflect the mind of Ignatius himself, set forth in the *Exercises,* in other writings, or in the "oral commentary" that has been handed on in the Jesuit order.

which he offered? Is there a benign interpretation which I can place on it? How can I favorably understand it?

If he cannot answer these questions satisfactorily to himself, he ought to go back to the man who made the suggestions and ask him these questions in a nonthreatening way. Thus, he will not harm his fellow-Christian and may derive some real profit for himself.

(It does not take an exegetical genius here to see an allusion to the petty persecution which Ignatius suffered in his lifetime. He suggests that Christians with "new ideas" ought to be treated gently: a suggestion not inappropriate for our age.)

Suggestions

(It is understood that the *Spiritual Exercises* as St. Ignatius wrote them are not assembled in a clearly cohesive book form. Rather, the whole book is a series of jottings. These were written down in large part by Father Ignatius himself and in some measure by fairly contemporary Jesuits. The book as it stands would be almost unintelligible if read by the beginner from cover to cover. Rather, the book has been understood by subsequent generations only because it was interpreted in light of a rather rich oral tradition which came down along with the book itself. In this paraphrase of the *Spiritual Exercises*, we are trying to interpolate some of that oral tradition. The first half of our book represents an amplification of the second half. The second half tries to present as much of the mind of Father Ignatius as can be gleaned from the jottings of the *Spiritual Exercises* and some of the oral commentary that accompanied them.)

The little book begins with a series of suggestions and the general theme of these suggestions is as follows:

The human body grows strong through exercise, whether by walking or swimming, running or the like. Men become more vigorous and healthy by using their God-given physical gifts. There is something similar in spiritual growth. While it is true that all spiritual growth is a gift of God, still it is generally His good pleasure that men grow spiritually in so far as they exercise the spiritual faculties which He has given them. And so I have come to call my booklet *Spiritual Exercises*, as it is intended to do for the soul, with God's grace, what gymnastics of any kind do for the human body. In connection with the above, the person who "guides" the spiritual exercises should understand that he is to do just that. There is no substitute for personal activity on the part of the person making the exercises—the exercitant. And therefore the director should be content simply to relate the gospel passage to be contemplated, to give a certain amount of background and some interpretation of scripture, and then to leave the exercitant, with the help of the Spirit, to make the meditation himself. It is the part of the exercitant really to do whatever work is to be done in the exercises. He must personally be much engaged or he will derive little profit. Finally, the exercitant himself should be content to meditate on a single point given by the director, if he finds that the Spirit enables him to find satisfaction in contemplating that single point. The exercises are not a text book that must be completed before the course is over!

In all of the meditations which follow, the exercitant ought to be very careful when he is speaking with the Divine Majesty to exercise great reverence even in his interior attitude. Generally speaking, the more generous and reverent one tries to show himself in his dealings with the Divinity, so much the more generous is the Divinity in dealing with the person who seeks Him.

I have divided the exercises into four weeks. Each "week" is simply a part of the exercises. The first portion is spent in consideration of the nature of sin; the second, the life of our Lord from the Incarnation to Palm Sunday. The third week is spent in contemplating the suffering of our Lord, and the fourth week is devoted to His resurrected life.

It should be carefully understood that the amount of time to be spent on each week of the exercises is by no means automatic. The beginner in the spiritual life may find it necessary to spend a great deal of time contemplating the nature of sin in general and his own personal past sins. The more proficient in the spiritual life may find it helpful to spend greater portions of time contemplating the life of our Lord as He lived it on earth, or in deriving necessary strength and support from contemplating the example of Christ's suffering or His glorious risen life. The decision to move from one week of the exercises to the next is not to be made lightly. Here, as shall be treated later in the book, the director must be very careful to attend to the movements of the Spirit and thus to assist the exercctitant in knowing when it is time for him to move on to a new area of contemplation.

When a person makes the exercises, he should attempt, in so far as frail human nature allows, to make them with the attitude of denying the Creator and Lord nothing that He clearly asks. The director of the exercises should inquire from time to time of the exercitant how things are going. He should ask what spiritual movements the exercitant finds in himself. He should inquire gently but firmly about the means which the exercitant is taking to make the exercises a profitable experience. If he finds that the exercitant is suffering from spiritual "dryness," he should treat him with special gentleness. In fact, this "dryness" can be a means of serving the Divine Majesty and the exercitant should attempt to accept it as coming from God's hand. If, on the other hand, he finds that the exercitant is receiving great consolation in prayer, the director should caution him in the manner in which this consolation is to be received. This point too will be developed further, at another point in our book.

When the exercitant is enjoying consolation in prayer it is easy to make the full hour of meditation. In times of dryness of course, this is much more difficult. For this reason, the exercitant ought to be encouraged in moments of dryness to attempt to spend some few extra moments in prayer and thus go counter to his weaker nature.

There is one danger of spiritual consolation, that under the force of it, the exercitant may make promises of life-long commitment which he really is not able to fulfill. The director should caution the exercitant against making such promises. Any ideas which come to the exercitant in moments of consolation should be re-examined frequently by the exercitant, with the aid of his director, in more sober light.

It is terribly important that the director should avoid pressuring the exercitant toward any decision, however laudable. Any serious conclusions on reform of life that are reached in the course of the exercises are to be the work of the Spirit, and secondarily of the exercitant. The director must attempt to keep himself neutral. Such neutrality will help to create a mood of tranquility which is generally required by the Spirit that he may work profitably in the hearts of men. But it may happen that an exercitant may realize, with the help of the Divine Majesty, that he is powerfully attracted to some material good and this for the wrong reason. He may find, for example, that he desires a particular position of power and influence not for good Christian motives, but through sheer love of prestige. In such cases, he ought to try sincerely to pray for the opposite, assuring the Divine Majesty that he would prefer to go without the position if it is to separate him from the Lord of all.

Without undue intrusion on the part of the director—for the sharing of confidences with a director is something that must rise spontaneously from the good-will of the exercitant and his feelings of trust towards the director,—it will be of great help if the director knows well the interior life of the exercitant, both his strengths and his weaknesses. Thus, he will be able more easily and profitably to help him.

Finally, insofar as is possible, the one making the exercises ought to withdraw himself from other affairs and from dealings with other men. If it is possible, the exercises ought to occupy one's full time and energy.

A First Principle

Man was created to praise God and to serve him in reverential fear. Thus is man to gain eternal salvation. All other things, except man himself, are created for man—to help him praise the Divinity. It follows logically, does it not, that a reasonable man will use all created things only insofar as they help him toward his proper goal. But this is not easy. Created goods have an attractiveness of their own which can distract us from their proper use. So a reasonable man must make himself *actively indifferent* to created things to the extent that, in theory, he would not desire good health rather than illness, wealth rather than want, esteem rather than contempt, longevity rather than premature death, until he sees in a concrete case which of these polarities leads him the more directly to the Divinity.

On Examination of Conscience

(The "particular" examination of conscience is integral to Ignatian spirituality. It involves concentration on the eradication of a lesser fault or the acquisition of a particular virtue over a period of some weeks. If Ignatius' words are not carefully studied, the process can look mechanical. It is not. Some of his practical psychology, such as the stress on *one day at a time* has found its way into such therapies as *Alcoholics Anonymous*.)

Immediately on rising, we should remind ourselves of the virtue we are stressing this day and ask the Lord of All for the grace to grow in it. After the noon day meal, we should again address the Creator and ask His help in examining our progress thus far. We should repeat this after the evening meal or just before retiring. The manner of each of these prayer-periods is as follows: First, we place ourselves most solemnly in the Divine presence and then we ask His grace to know ourselves as He knows us. For a moment or two, we reflect on our faults as He reveals them to us. Then we devote ourselves to minutes of sincere repentance and ask the grace needed to improve in the future.

Some find it helpful to keep a daily record in a notebook, drawing a longer line for progress in a virtue or lack of progress with a given fault according to a kind of private shorthand. One's progress may then be easily examined over a period of days.

(Note in the above that the actual examination of conscience takes but a moment or two. The rest of the time is devoted to simple communion with God in prayer.)

Thought, Word, and Deed

(Ignatius devotes some time to examining varieties and degrees of sinfulness that can be present in thought, in speech, in deed. Perhaps some who write in areas of moral theology today, might wish to quarrel with Ignatius on certain points. But Ignatius is writing here for those who wish to be perfect. For such, all areas of human activity must grow more and more subservient to the Will of the Divinity.)

A General Confession

On the occasion of The Exercises, it may be useful to make a common confession of one's past life. It may help to attaining proper sorrow for our past sins, if we reflect on them all at once; it may help us to a deeper knowledge of ourselves and prepare us for a more meaningful reception of the Eucharist.

(Many confessors today would be very hesitant to endorse this suggestion. In any event, it is probably not applicable to one making the *Exercises* as we are, outside of a religious house and separated from a large supply of talented confessors.)

An Exercise in Meditation

(One sometimes reads about the Ignatian method of prayer, and that generally in a context of disparagement. Actually, Ignatius taught a variety of methods. Even the word "method" is not acceptable to some persons. Themselves gifted in prayer, they feel that any method runs the risk of restricting easy movement. It should be stressed, however, that in his exercises—as he called them—Fr. Ignatius concerns himself with the person who is only moderately gifted with talent for prayer. Coaches in various athletic endeavors generally ignore the supremely gifted—the supremely gifted will succeed in any event—when devising instruction. For the athlete of medium gifts, a certain method, regularity and fidelity to a modicum of prescriptions generally bears fruit.)

We begin by making a simple prayer to God that all our actions in the time of prayer may serve only the praise and service of His Divine Majesty.

As a preamble we make a *compositio* with our imaginations. This is an image in the mind that is associated with the subject of our prayer. If we become distracted or restless during our prayer, it is helpful to return to this image for a few moments. It serves as a kind of focus for our prayer.

One kind of *compositio* will differ from another. When we are contemplating the life of Christ, we simply present to our imaginations an image of the Temple where Christ was presented or the mountainside on which he seated himself while teaching. In a meditation on an abstract subject, like the Nature of Sin, we must create a picture that has something to do with the subject under reflection.

For example, conscious of the driving forces of our passions that may destroy us if they are not properly channelled, we might think of the soul of man as a human forced to live among brute beasts.

A second *preamble* is to pray to the Lord that we may attain the precise goal of a given meditation. We should be specific here. We should know what we are doing. For example, in praying about the Resurrection, we ask for a deep share of the joy of the Risen Lord. In contemplating the sufferings of the Lord, we ask for a share of His interior feelings and for shame on our own part that our sins were involved in His suffering.

Before any meditation, we ought to observe these three preliminaries: a basic prayer offering our moments to the Lord, a *compositio* that our imaginations may help us, and a prayer directed toward the goal of a specific meditation.

A Meditation on Sin

We use our memory to recall the first sin: that of the Angels. We bring our intelligence to bear on it by thinking out all the implications of this sin and its results. This action of our memory and understanding will lead to movements of our will. First the will shall desire that we be filled with feelings of shame, contemplating the punishment which the angels merited through a single sin. Though I have committed many sins, I have not been so punished. Then, too, we reflect that angels, as were we, were created as free creatures, but with a goal of offering reverential fear and service to the Divine Majesty. They ended badly, moving from humility to pride and from grace to destruction. Reflecting thus and in other ways as the spirit may move, we present all this to the will that it may respond.

We proceed in a like manner with the sin of Adam and Eve, calling to mind the event and reflecting soberly on its consequences to the whole human family. We see that they too were created in grace, but chose destruction. The consequences of their act we present to ourselves as the occasion for sober intellectual reflection. We desire that the results of that reflection should influence our wills.

Then we reflect on a third theoretical possibility, that of a mortal who committed a single serious sin and through it was separated irrevocably from the Creator of All. We reflect on this with the full force of the intellect so as to influence our wills.

A Conversation

We imagine Christ to be present and on the cross. We speak to him. We ask him to explain how, as Lord of All, he came to be a creature, how and why he came from eternal life to temporal death—and to a death precisely for my sins. We listen. We ask ourselves then: what have I done for Christ? What am I doing for Christ? What ought I to do for Christ?

We carry on this conversation—and subsequent ones—as one friend speaks to another or as a servant to his master: seeking now a favor, now acknowledging a fault, now making all one's affairs open to the other that one may be advised. Again we listen. Then we close this prayer with the Our Father.

A Second Meditation on Sin

The preparatory prayer is the same as in the meditation preceding. The *compositio* is the same.

We ask for what we truly desire. Here we petition the Lord of All for a deep interior sorrow for our sins.

We divide our reflection then into five points for consideration:

1. We try to recall, at least in outline, all the sins of our past lives, examining our lives year by year and place by place. It may be useful to call to mind each of the places where we dwelled for any length of time, our relationships with other persons, the office or state of life in which we lived from one year or one decade to the next.

2. We reflect on the innate evil nature of sin, how destructive sin is, how unworthy a given sinful action of man would be even if it were not forbidden.

3. I reflect on my own small place in the universe. Who am I in comparison with the whole living human family? Who are they in comparison with all the angels and the elect who dwell now with God in Heaven? What is all creation in comparison with the Divine Majesty? In this chain then, who am I that have rebelled against the Lord of All?

4. We reflect on the nature of the God against Whom I have sinned. I compare His attributes with mine: His wisdom with my ignorance, His omnipotence with my weakness, His justice with my injustice, His goodness with my sinfulness.

5. I reflect then on the restraint of all created nature in dealing with me. The angels, though frequently the swords of Divine Justice, have protected me and prayed for me. The sun, the moon, and the stars have not fallen on me but warmed me and lighted my path. The earth has not swallowed me up alive but has supported my feet and brought forth food for my body.

I conclude then, beginning a conversation with the Lord of All. I express my gratitude that He has given me life in which I may repent. I promise most solemnly to amend my future life—with the gift of His grace. And I end the conversation by reciting the Our Father.

A Threefold Conversation

I may at some later time repeat the preceding meditation, dwelling on points that I found profitable or difficult when I made the meditation the first time.

Then I finish the meditation with a threefold conversation.

First, I speak with Our Lady and ask her to obtain the grace from her Son and Lord that I may have a deep interior knowledge of my sins and a hatred of them; that I may perceive the spiritual disorder which underlies much of my actions and that, having become aware of it, I may watch my actions more carefully. Finally I ask for a knowledge of what it means to be "worldly," that I may move myself away from "worldly" actions and ambitions.

Then I so speak with our Lord Jesus Christ.

Finally, I speak similarly with God the Father, that the Lord of All may grant these requests to me.

Again, I recite the Our Father.

A Meditation on Hell

The usual preparatory prayers are made.

Compositio Here it is to see with the imagination the length and breadth and depth of Hell itself.

The second preamble is to ask for what I really want. Here it is to obtain a real understanding of what the souls in Hell suffer, so that if I should ever become forgetful of the Love of God, at least the fear of punishment would keep me from sin.

1. The first point is to imagine the fire of Hell with massive tongues of flame and the lost souls themselves composed, as it were, of bodies made of fire.
2. Second, to hear the cries and shouts of the damned, their blasphemies against the Lord Christ and against His saints.
3. To smell the odor of burning pitch and putrescence.
4. To taste the bitterness of tears, sadness, and relentless conscience.
5. To attempt to feel the burning flames themselves.

Then we begin a conversation with the Lord Christ, reflecting on the kinds of persons who might have found their way into hell. Some might have fallen for lack of belief; others believed but did not act. Some may have been damned for mistakes before the coming of Christ; other damned souls lived as his contemporaries; others lived long after Him.

Finally, I thank Him that I am not already among the numbers of the damned, through his love and grace.

I finish the meditation with an Our Father.

Practical Helps for Making a Meditation

1. On retiring in the evening and before falling asleep, for the space of a Hail Mary, I remind myself of the hour when I am to rise and the subject on which I am to meditate.

2. Immediately on rising, I give myself to the thought of the upcoming period of prayer. In this case, I attempt to rouse in my soul feelings of shame for my many sins by presenting imaginative examples. I ask myself, for example, how a knight might feel in the presence of the king he had betrayed, especially if their meeting were to take place in the presence of the king's entire court. I should so imagine myself then in the presence of the King of All, surrounded by his entire heavenly court. I ask myself, how ought I to feel in this presence, since I have received so many favors and benefits from the Lord and have responded so badly.

3. Standing one or two steps away from the place in which I am to make my meditation, I acknowledge that I am about to enter, in a special way, into the presence of the Divine Majesty. I attempt to stir up some measure of the proper humility and respect.

4. The posture of prayer—kneeling, sitting, or lying prostrate—is simply determined by the results. If I find it useful to kneel, I do so. If I pray better standing, then of course I stand up. Moreover, I do not move to complete all the "points" of the meditation. If I find useful fruit in a single point, I stay with it for the entire hour of prayer.

5. Sometime after the meditation is over, I reflect on the manner in which I made it, asking myself if I honestly could have done more for the success of the hour. What

precisely could I have done? And then I thank the Lord
for the opportunity of having prayed.

6. Apart from the times of prayer, I try to keep a mood
that is commensurate with the "week" of the exercises:
stirring up in myself a genuine regret and repentance as
a mood of the first week, or a special joy as the mood of
the fourth week.

7. Penance is useful too. One may call *internal* penance the
effort to feel a real interior sorrow for my sins. External
penance may be useful, as in fasting. It is not fasting to
take away what is superfluous. That is merely temper-
ance. Rather penance here is to do without that which is
in some measure "necessary." There is little to be gained
by fasting to the point where one does not have the
strength to pray. Here too, we must seek *that which we
truly desire*: in this case, a degree of penance that aids
our prayer and does not hinder it.

We should deal in the same manner with sleep. To cut
down on superfluous sleep is not penance. On the other
hand, to do with so little sleep as to be constantly tired
and irritable is not wisdom.

Penance has several values. In the divine plan, it can
atone for sin, through the merits of the Lord Christ. It
contributes to the strengthening of the will, as the lower
forces of the person are made to yield to the higher. Most
important, if joined to the proper interior dispositions, it
can aid toward increasing our feelings of sadness and regret
for sin and enable us to empathize with the sufferings of
the Lord Christ during His Passion here on earth.

Sometimes in these matters a little experimentation is
called for if we do not obtain *what we truly desire*. We

may try more penance, rather than less or vice versa; we may try a different kind of penance, or a variety of penances until the desired effect is attained. But real prudence is called for in these matters and the advice of the director here should generally be heeded, as the likelihood of self-delusion here is great. Still, the Lord of All knows us far better than we know ourselves. These experimentations give us the opportunity to perceive His will for us in the results, if we look for that will very honestly.

Finally, during time of retreat, it is helpful to exercise our particular examination of conscience   precisely on our fidelity to these practical helps.

The Second Week

The Call of the Temporal King
An Aid to Contemplating the Life of the Eternal King

The usual preparatory prayer is made.

The *compositio* is to imagine the synagogues, the towns, and villages where the Lord Christ preached.

Our prayer then is that we may not be deaf to the call of Christ, but prompt and ready to do the divine will.

1. We imagine an ideal human king, chosen by God Himself, to whom all are to show honor and respect.
2. The King speaks: it is my firm intention to free the world from the infidel. All who wish to come with me must be satisfied with the same food and clothing that I shall use. They must work as I shall work, do without sleep, as I shall often do without sleep. Our victory however is assured. All will then share the fruits of that victory

with me, even as they have borne with me the burden of
the struggle.
3. Consider what any human response would be to such a
king, so generous, so beneficent. Consider how mean-
spirited would be the response of any person who was
not interested in participating.

The second part of this meditation is to realize that the
"ideal king" is but a symbol·for Jesus Christ to whom all
the points of the comparison apply.

Christ calls us to make the whole world deeply
Christian. Thus will Christ "enter into the glory of the
Father" and we with Him. Who suffers with Him will
surely share the glory with Him.

All noble-minded men will surely respond to such a call.
Some however will desire to serve in the front-ranks of
such an army, where the pain and the toil are the greatest.
In addition to the demands which Christian life imposes,
these persons will wish to do more and they will pray:

*Eternal Lord of all things, with your help and grace I make
this offering. In the presence of Your Infinite Goodness and in
the sight of the glorious Virgin, your Mother, I assure you that
it is my most solemn desire—provided that it be for your
greater service and praise—to live as you lived, to imitate you
in bearing all injuries and contempt, to live in spiritual poverty
and actual deprivation—if the Divine Majesty should so call
me.*

(It is clear that the recitation of this prayer involves an
awesome amount of sanctity. Generations of would-be
disciples of Fr. Ignatius have stumbled here. Some because
they could not recite the prayer and walked sadly away.

Others because they recited the prayer without realizing that they were not called to recite it, that the Spirit, as we remarked in Part I was not about to "underwrite" their reciting it. Some of these disciples ended badly. Ignatius himself, when interviewing candidates for the Jesuit order, would ask them if they "desired" to be able to make this prayer. When many said no, he would ask them if they at least "desired the desire" to be able to make it. Under this rubric and with a humbling vision of the limits of their sanctity, many men were admitted to Jesuit ranks.)

This meditation should be made twice, once in the morning and once before the evening meal.

During the second week, it may be useful to do some reading, as from the Imitation of Christ, the gospels, or the lives of the saints.

The Incarnation

The usual preparatory prayer is made.

Then a brief "history of the event" is brought to mind. The Trinity is seen reflecting from all eternity on the problems of man's salvation. Thus was made the eternal decree that the second person of the Trinity would become man. In the fullness of time the angel Gabriel is sent to the Virgin.

Compositio Here it will be to imagine the size of the whole world in which the men live—whom Jesus has come to save. Then we are to imagine the house and chamber of the Virgin in Nazareth of the province of Galilee.

Then I must ask for what I really desire. Here it is an intimate knowledge of the Lord, who became man for me. I wish to know him deeply so that I shall wish to follow him.

1. To imagine all the men on the face of the earth at the time of the Incarnation. What diversity! How they differ in clothing and in customs! Some are white and others black. Some are at peace and others in war. Some are in tears and others in laughter. Some are sick, while others enjoy good health. Some are being born even as others die. And all are in need of salvation.

2. To consider the three persons of the Most Holy Trinity. To see that they are observing the condition of man and seeing how hopeless it would be without the Saviour.

3. To observe the persons on the face of the earth. To hear them. To see how much they are in need of redemption. Then we must try to hear the Persons of the Trinity decreeing redemption. Then we try to hear the conversation between Our Lady and the angel. Finally, we try to reflect on all that we have heard and to draw profit from it.

4. To consider the actions of the human persons, their crimes against one another and against the Trinity. To reflect on the actions of the Trinity. To reflect on the actions of the angel and Our Lady. He acts as God's emissary. She humbles herself before him and gives thanks. Then we try to consider all this deeply so as to draw profit from it.

Finally, I begin a series of conversations. What ought I to say to the three Divine Persons? What should I say to the Eternal Word? What to Our Lady and His mother?

Each of us should ask—as the Spirit teaches him—to learn what will aid in following and imitating the Lord Christ, Who has become Incarnate. We conclude by saying: Our Father.

The Nativity

The usual preparatory prayer is made.

The next preparatory point is the history of the event. Here it is the departure of Our Lady from Nazareth. She is nearly nine months pregnant. She rides on a donkey, accompanied by Joseph and a servant girl. They journey to Bethlehem to pay tribute which had been imposed by Caesar.

Compositio To imagine the journey from Nazareth to Bethlehem. To wonder what the road was like, narrow or broad, steep or sloping, through valleys or over mountains. (Since Ignatius himself had lived in the Holy Land and doubtless traveled this route, he has something other in mind than a question in biblical geography. However one forms a mental image of this route, the image then must become firmly fixed in the imagination. This is likely to happen, Ignatius felt, if one decides for himself whether the road was broad or narrow.) To imagine the cave. Was it deep or not? How was it furnished?

The first point is to see the persons: Our Lady, Joseph, the servant girl, and finally—the infant Jesus who is born for my sake. I look on these persons and see their needs. As though I were present, I approach them with all possible reverence. I reflect on who they are.

Then I listen to the persons and think about what they are saying.

Finally, I reflect on what these persons have done. It was this: They made a journey that the Lord might be born in deepest poverty and—after a life of toil, of hunger and thirst, of heat and cold, injuries and contempt—that finally he might die on the cross and *all this for me.*

I think about these things and attempt to draw profit. I conclude with a conversation as in the preceding meditation. Then I recite the Our Father.

(It is sometimes said of Robert Southwell's Christmas poem, "The Burning Babe," that it is unique, as it combines the thoughts of Christmas and the Passion. Southwell, apparently, was not the first Jesuit to have the idea.)

On Using the Five Senses in Prayer

(Ignatius sometimes speaks of *applicatio sensuum*. As will be seen, this is the use of the imagination with a special emphasis.)

We shall use our imaginations in a special way to review the material of the last two meditations.

1. To see the persons with the vision of the imagination, trying to watch them in the particular circumstances described in the last two meditations.

2. To hear what they say, and to derive spiritual profit from it.

3. To smell and to taste the odor of Divine Goodness, the special beauty of the soul and its virtues.

4. To touch and embrace and kiss at least the places where these persons were.

This exercise too is ended in a conversation with the persons involved in the meditation. Then we recite the Our Father.

Further Suggestions

During this week of the exercises, I may review meditations already done but I should not think of a mystery from Christ's life which has not yet been the subject of prayer. As the time of prayer approaches, I should make a special effort to focus my attention on precisely the one mystery of the meditation.

It may be useful to make the first meditation, the Incarnation, at midnight, a second time at dawn, and a third time at the hour of Mass, a fourth time at Vespers and a fifth time before supper. Each of these meditations should last about an hour.

If the exercitant is not physically strong, the midnight meditation might be fitted in during the day and the exercitant's sleep not interrupted.

In this week, the exercitant should keep before himself one main idea: I wish to know the Incarnate Word better and better that I may serve him more diligently and follow him more closely.

A Consideration

Christ gave us the example. He lived in a human family and was obedient to His parents. Listening, however, to the command of His Heavenly Father He separated Himself from His adoptive father and His natural mother and remained in the Temple; thus He opened Himself totally to the service of the Divine Majesty. We are in the process of contemplating His life. While contemplating it, we may ask the Father to show us in what state of life we are to carry out our service to the Lord. As a preparation for contemplating the answer to that question, the following meditation may be useful.

The Two Banners

The usual preparatory prayer is made.

The first prelude is the narrative. Here it is simply to recall that Christ wishes to gather all men under a single banner, while Lucifer wishes rather to gather men under his banner.

The *compositio* is to see the place. Christ gathers His followers in a field near Jerusalem while Lucifer gathers his near Babylon.

Then we ask what we truly desire. Here it is an intimate knowledge of the cruel fraud and delusion which Satan offers and an equally deep knowledge of the peace and love and joy to which Christ calls. We ask for grace to heed that call.

We consider how Satan sends his minions out into every town and city, province and village, missing none. They do not forget to visit a single place, a single state of life, a single person.

We listen to Satan's instructions. He urges his army to lure men on—teaching them to love the riches of this life, that they may become fond of honors, and thus be led to pride. Satan stresses and underlines the progression: wealth, honors, pride. All his other delusions and wiles are but variants on these themes.

We compare this to Christ.

Even the locale is different. The field near Jerusalem is a pleasant place, filled with wild flowers.

Christ calls disciples and apostles, persons of every stripe, and sends them too to every village and province, ignoring no state, no person. They are to carry His teaching.

We see how Christ deals with His servants and friends. How gentle He is with them!

He speaks to them. He explains how they are to call men to spiritual poverty—at least to a genuine detachment from material goods—and to a desire of actual want and deprivation, if it be the Father's will. They are to call also for a desire of abuse and contempt—that Christians may arrive at humility.

The two teachings are in flat opposition: poverty against wealth, contempt against honor, pride against humility. Poverty, a love of contempt, and humility—all other Christian virtues, says Jesus, can be subordinated to these.

I begin a conversation with Our Lady that she may obtain the grace from her Son that I be received under His banner, that I may come to love at least spiritual poverty and may even feel deprivation—if God so will. I pray that I may experience contempt—if it can be without offense to the Divine Majesty. And I recite a Hail Mary.

I pray similarly to the Son that He may intercede with the Father. And I recite the *Anima Christi.*

I speak so with the Father and ask these gifts. Then I recite the Our Father.

This exercise is to be made twice—once at midnight and once in early morning. (Again, the awesome holiness which the Exercises has as its goal is bluntly stated here. "Let those accept it who can!" Mt. 19.12. Two errors are to be avoided here. One is a cavalier dismissal of the possibility that I am called to such heights; another is a reckless climbing of the mountain without heeding to see if the Spirit truly calls. Neither error will lead to sanctity, though the latter may cause more problems than the former. We must attempt to be totally open to the Spirit and to follow where He leads.)

(Much of the rest of this week of the *Exercises* is occupied with contemplations on the public life of Christ before the Passion. For the beginner in meditative prayer, Ignatius' outlines are, perhaps, not useful since they are quite stark and need development. To some extent, of course, this was done in Part I of this book. Still, two examples may be interesting.)

The Flight into Egypt
(Mt. 2.13-18)

1. Herod wished to murder the child Jesus and he did slay the Holy Innocents. But Joseph was forewarned: Rise, take the child and his mother and flee into Egypt.

2. He rose and went into Egypt.

3. He was there until the death of Herod.

The Life of Christ From the Age of Twelve to Thirty
(Lk. 2.51-52)

1. He was obedient to his parents. He grew in Wisdom and Age and grace.

2. He seems to have worked as a carpenter as Mark 6. says: Is this not the carpenter?

(Whether the range of these meditations is to be limited to the points Ignatius makes or whether the scriptural passages are to be opened up for further consideration is disputed among scholars who write on the *Exercises*. Ignatius' book of the *Exercises* has some ten pages of meditation outlines like the above.)

On Humility

(Ignatius seems almost obsessed with this concept. He returns to it repeatedly in what is, after all, a very short book. The word means many things to many people. Perhaps a descriptive definition of the way Ignatius uses the term could be: a proper understanding of the relationship between God and man.)

Three Varieties of Humility

1. The first is that which is necessary for salvation. I have a fixed purpose never, in a serious way, to offend the Divine Majesty no matter what the bribe or threat. I shall not offend if I am offered the sum total of all created goods or am threatened with the loss of life. Never will I seriously violate God's law.
2. This is a more perfect form. I would not offend the Divinity in a minor matter for any bribe or threat. As a general condition which makes this possible, I really do not prefer wealth to poverty, a cheerful old age to premature death, or honor to disgrace—if the service of God is equal in one case or the other.
3. The third is perfection. All other things being equal, the glory of God and the good of souls, I would prefer deprivation and contempt with the poor and condemned Christ to any combination of wealth and honor

which the world offers. Poverty with Christ Who was poor, contempt with Christ Who was despised—these are my earnest desires.

It will be useful for one who wishes to arrive at the third stage to carry on three conversations: with Our Lady, Our Lord Christ, and the Heavenly Father, earnestly asking the grace to be called to the ranks of them that live in the third state.

(This is it: the apex of the Exercises and perhaps of Christian perfection. Everything prior in the Exercises has led up to this: all that follows is to give the Exercitant the strength personally to arrive at this point.)

On Making Decisions

Since the goal and purpose of the Exercises is the making of decisions, a discussion of decision-making is much in order. First, the ultimate guiding light of our decision should be that we are creatures, created for a special purpose. Any serious decision should be made in light of that purpose. Nor should I confuse a final goal with a means or vice versa. For example, some men think of a particular potential wife first and only then do they consider matrimony. Rather the well-ordered man would settle the question, "Is it the will of the Divine Majesty that I should get married?" and then, if he reached a positive conclusion, would he begin to look for a wife. Others choose first to seek some high ecclesiastical office and having attained it, wonder how best they may serve God in that office. They ought to have asked themselves originally, "Is it the will of the Divine Majesty that I should serve Him in such an office?" In other words, the only serious consideration in making a decision is whether one choice or its opposite will lead to a greater service of God and the good of souls.

We must then be *indifferent*, cheerfully accepting X or non-X once it is clear which leads to God's greater service. There are some things of course that are beyond the realm of choice: if we are engaged in a valid Christian marriage, we may not choose whether to remain married or not. Any choice then must be within the framework of our obligation to remain married.

How Are Decisions Made?

One way is perhaps the best of all. God so sweetly yet powerfully moves the soul that it reaches out—freely but without doubt—to the proper choice. So did St. Matthew and St. Paul come to follow the Lord Christ. The second is much like the first; the soul is so filled with light and grace and peace that the intellect sees the proper choice easily, although without dramatic divine intervention; as in the case of Paul, or the actual physical presence of Christ, as in the case of Matthew.

The third manner is the one that is generally open to us. In a tranquil mood, when the soul is at peace, the person, motivated by the desire of serving and praising the Lord of All, calmly examines the reasons *pro* and *contra* a given choice. He may even write them down on a piece of paper and look at them.

In so making a choice, there are some steps to be followed:

1. I should know what is the subject under discussion, precisely what the decision-making is about. I am deliberating about X, not about Y or Z.
2. I must be conscious of my created purpose. I must make myself incline neither for nor against a particular decision until I see how it fits the purpose for which I was created.
3. I must seek from the Lord of All that He move my will, that He incline me only to that which is fitting to my final goal, illuminating my intellect that I may see and my will that I may choose that which is His Will for me.
4. Then I reflect, in great calmness now, examining those arguments which support the judgment that decision X will lead me better to my final goal. Similarly do I examine the arguments against such a conclusion.
5. I see calmly where my intellect is leading me. I accept the conclusion.
6. With much prayer, I present this conclusion to the Lord of All. I seek again His light and instruction.

Rules for Distinguishing Between
Influences in the Soul—Good and Bad

1. It is generally the part of the Divinity or his angel to bring peace and joy to the soul, entering easily and gracefully without distress. In fact, they remove whatever distress they may find. Satan however is usually violent in his entrance and brings turbulence and distress in his wake, routing out what peace he finds through skill of argumentation.
2. God alone can delight the soul without visible cause –I

mean without prior perceptible reason. When the soul moves from distress or passivity to intense spiritual joy and no cause, no reason, no argument can be found, such joy can only be of God.

3. Both the good and evil angel can bring happiness to the soul—but from different goals. The good angel that he may lead the soul from the good to the better; the evil spirit desires, of course, to lead the soul from the good to the worse.

4. The evil spirit is quite capable of disguising himself as a good angel, entering a pious soul with thoughts that are congruent to piety and then gradually shifting his ground so as to bring the soul to destruction.

5. We ought to try and keep track of the progression of our spiritual thoughts. If in their beginning, middle, and end, they lead us to the good, then we may conclude that they are the work of a good spirit. But if in their progress an element of disquiet is introduced and poor effects result, we may conclude that this was the work of the evil spirit, no matter how good the beginning appeared to be.

6. When the above happens and we have detected the footprints, as it were, of the evil spirit who has robbed us of our tranquility, we ought to review the whole sequence of events in our thinking. Thus, perhaps, we can detect precisely how he made his entrance and be forewarned for the future.

7. In persons who are generally disposed to the good, the angel moves with ease and the evil spirit with considerable discomfort. *E contra,* in persons with bad habits and a kind of disposition to that which is evil, the evil spirit moves easily and the good spirit has difficulties. For our purposes, then, a person who is generally disposed to the good can frequently tell the difference be-

tween movements from the Good and movements from the Evil, if he perceives the manner of their entrance.

8. Spiritual consolation without prior cause (a perceptible thought, an object, an action) can only come from God—as we have said. Still the deeply spiritual person who believes he has received such consolation should always be alert. First, because he may not have noticed the prior cause, and secondly because the evil spirit is capable of moving in the wake even of such God-given consolation and using it for his own purposes.

The Third Week I

The usual preparatory prayer is made.

The second prelude is to relate the narrative briefly to oneself.

Our Lord sent two disciples into Jerusalem to prepare supper. Then He came Himself with the remaining disciples. After He had eaten the paschal lamb, He washed the disciples' feet. He gave them then His most sacred body, His precious blood. He taught them at some length. Judas went out then to betray the Lord.

The *compositio* is to see the place. Here it is the way from Bethany to Jerusalem. Is it narrow or wide, steep or sloping? We look at the room of the supper and decide what it looks like.

Then we ask what we really desire. Here it is sorrow, shame, and grief with the suffering Christ who goes to His Passion for my sins.

1. I try to see the persons at the supper and by reflecting on them I attempt to derive spiritual profit.
2. I listen to what they are saying.
3. I watch what they are doing.
4. I consider the sufferings that the Lord Christ endures

and wishes to endure. I attempt to rouse in myself suitable feelings of grief and compassion.

5. I consider how the Divinity conceals itself. Capable of destroying all enemies the Divinity does not. Rather, the sacred humanity is permitted to suffer most cruelly.

6. I consider that all this suffering is for me and my sins. I ask what I ought to do, how I ought to suffer in return.

I say the Our Father.

I am alert in the conversations which I begin with the suffering Christ. I advert to the feelings I find within myself of pain and grief—or lack thereof— and discuss all these with Christ.

If the Spirit so moves me, I may conclude with three conversations—as at the end of the Meditation on the Two Banners—with the Virgin, the Lord Christ, and the Heavenly Father.

The Third Week II

The usual preparararatory prayer is made.

The narrative is briefly recited. The Lord Christ comes down from Mount Sion, where the supper had taken place, accompanied now by eleven disciples. He comes to the Valley of Josephat. He leaves eight disciples and leads the remaining three into an inner garden. He falls into deep prayer. Through deep anxiety, he sweats, apparently, drops of blood. Three times he prays to the Father, and stirs the three disciples from sleep. His enemies fall at the sound of His voice. Judas kisses Him. Peter cuts off the ear of Malchus but Christ heals him. He is taken as a common criminal and dragged out of the valley to the house of Annas.

The *compositio* is to see the place. I consider the way from Sion to the valley of Josephat and the garden. Were these place broad or narrow, steep or sloping?

I ask what I truly desire. Here it is a share in the passion, agony with Christ Who agonizes, grief, pain, tears, and deep internal sorrow for the great burden which Christ has borne for me.

Again I ask myself the question: who are these persons? what are they doing? what are they saying? what does it mean? And I discuss all these things with the Virgin, with Christ, with the Heavenly Father.

All the rules we have explained until now are to be observed during the third week, such as bringing the subject of prayer to mind as soon as we awake, preparing ourselves immediately before prayer to enter the divine presence, etc.

Depending on one's spiritual and physical strength, this one meditation above may be made five times or fewer in a single day.

I must avoid cheerful thoughts during the third week, even if they have to do with the gospel message, such as thoughts of the Resurrection and of Heaven. I must try to keep a general frame of mind during these days that is occupied with pain and sorrow with the Christ that suffers— for my sins.

For one who is making the full exercises, the following schedule may be followed:

One day is devoted to the events from the garden to the house of Annas, from the house of Annas to that of

Caiphas. These meditations are repeated then with a special stress on the use of the senses in imagination.

A day is devoted to the events from the house of Caiphas, to that of Pilate and from Pilate to Herod.

A full day is devoted to the later events before Pilate.

A full day is devoted to the Crucifixion.

A full day is devoted to the events after Christ's death and up to His burial.

A full day is devoted to reviewing all the events of the Passion.

(In an appendix, Ignatius gives skeletal outlines of these meditations, using a format like that we demonstrated before in the second week.)

The Fourth Week

The Appearance of the Risen Lord to the Blessed Virgin

This was the first appearance of our Lord after the Resurrection. To be sure, it is recorded nowhere in the gospels, but there are some things that Scripture feels we ought to be intelligent enough to figure out for ourselves. After all, the Scriptures do say: "Are you without any intelligence?" (Mt. 16.9).

(Later exegetes note that an appearance to the Blessed

Virgin would not be recorded as it would be without any legal witness value, according to rabbinical norms. Some may like Ignatius' explanation better!)

The usual preparatory prayer is made.

The narrative is briefly recited. Christ died on the cross. His Holy soul descends into the nether regions and delivers the souls of the just. Thence, His soul returns to the tomb and rejoins the body. Body and soul appear to the Blessed Virgin.

The *compositio* is to see the places: The tomb and how it was arranged. Similarly we gaze at the home of the Virgin, her bedroom, the corner of the house that she used for prayer, etc.

Then I ask for what I really want: a share in the intense joy of the Christ that is Risen.

The first three points of the meditation are a familiar technique now: we look at the persons in these meetings, we see what they do, we listen to what they say. We pray that we may derive profit from this.

The fourth point is to see how triumphantly the Divine reveals itself.

The fifth to see how Christ exercises the role of *consoler* and to compare it with the way in which friends are consoled by friends.

To conclude with one or many conversations (Christ, the Virgin, God the Father) and to recite the Our Father.

Through the rest of the fourth week, we proceed analogously as we did in the third week. We may devote an entire day to the appearances to Magdalene, to Peter, to the disciples on Emmaus road, to the unbelieving Thomas, and to Joseph of Arimathea—as we may read in the lives of the saints. Then a day may be devoted to the Ascension of Our Lord.

A Contemplation to Increase Our Love for God

We start with two basic principles. First, love is shown by actions, not by promises. Secondly, it is the part of every lover to wish to share with the beloved, to bestow on the beloved, something the lover has, whether it is only an external thing such as wealth or honors or something a bit more internal such as knowledge. Each lover wishes to give to the beloved that which is his. If it were possible, any lover would really wish to give to the beloved that which he is, truly to give himself.

The *compositio* is to see Christ interceding for me with the Heavenly Father, seated in His court and surrounded by all the angels and saints who intercede for me also.

I pray for what I really want: a deep, living consciousness of the goods that the Divinity has constantly thrust on me that I may be properly motivated to serve and love the Divine Majesty as I ought.

1. I think of Creation itself, material creation and the new creation of Redemption, and how the Creator has tried to communicate His very life to me. I pray that I may be filled with the deep emotion that is reasonable in the face of such generosity. And I pray:

   Father, take all that I have, all that I am. Memory, understanding, freedom,—all these you gave me. Take them back. May all these gifts act and live only in accord with your most Holy Will. Grant me, though, your love and grace and these in abundance. If I have these, I do not want anything else. I pray in Jesus' name.

2. I note how God lives and acts in His creatures. In the very elements of life, that they may *be*, in vegetative life, that it may *grow*, in animal life, that it may *feel* in human life, that we may *understand*. To the extent that I am and grow and feel and understand, He is with me always. I am His temple, a reflection and image of His Eternal Beauty.

3. I reflect how God, as it were, *toils* in all created things—for my benefit. Sun and moon and stars, flocks of the field and crops of the earth flourish as He lives with them, keeping them in existence, in growth, and in feeling.

4. I reflect on the manner in which all these beautiful things descend from Infinite Goodness to me. I ask myself: how ought I to respond? I discuss all these things in conversation with the Father and I close with the Our Father.

(If there is any consolation for one who writes a book of this nature, it is this: Prayer is one of the few things in this life that is so valuable that to learn a little about it is infinitely preferable to not having learned at all.)